Fifth Workshop on Computational Linguistics for Literature 2016

Held at the 2016 Conference of the North American Chapter of the Association for Computational Linguistics: Human Language Technologies (NAACL HLT 2016)

San Diego, California, USA
16 June 2016

ISBN: 978-1-5108-2528-4

Printed from e-media with permission by:

Curran Associates, Inc.
57 Morehouse Lane
Red Hook, NY 12571

Some format issues inherent in the e-media version may also appear in this print version.

Copyright© (2016) by the Association for Computational Linguistics
All rights reserved.

Printed by Curran Associates, Inc. (2016)

For permission requests, please contact the Association for Computational Linguistics
at the address below.

Association for Computational Linguistics
209 N. Eighth Street
Stroudsburg, Pennsylvania 18360

Phone: 1-570-476-8006
Fax: 1-570-476-0860

acl@aclweb.org

Additional copies of this publication are available from:

Curran Associates, Inc.
57 Morehouse Lane
Red Hook, NY 12571 USA
Phone: 845-758-0400
Fax: 845-758-2634
Email: curran@proceedings.com
Web: www.proceedings.com

NAACL HLT 2016

**The 2016 Conference of the
North American Chapter of the
Association for Computational Linguistics:
Human Language Technologies**

**Proceedings of the Fifth Workshop
on Computational Linguistics for Literature**

June 16, 2016
San Diego, California, USA

Preface

Welcome to the fifth (yes!) edition of the Workshop on Computational Linguistics for Literature, aptly nicknamed CLfL. We started our workshops as a venue for computational linguists who had an interest in processing literary texts. That somewhat underspecified, and a slightly narrow, mandate has evolved over the next four years. A rather special research community has emerged, with NLP people alongside researchers in Digital Humanities, literary scholars, poets and more. You can trace a brief history of CLfL at its latest Web site.[1]

As a token of growing maturity of our workshop series, in October 2015 a special journal issue appeared, volume 12 of *Linguistic Issues in Language Technology*,[2] with expanded versions of several papers from the CLfL workshops held in 2012-2014.

Before we tell you about the program, a big thank-you. As usual, we owe a debt of gratitude to our excellent program committee, some of whom have been with us all these years. Their hard work ensures the high quality of papers. Their dedication, passion and insights are greatly appreciated!

This year the participants will be entertained and maybe intrigued by a nicely varied program.

The workshop exists in the "twilight zone" between computation and art. Our distinguished invited speakers highlight this duality. The morning speaker is Professor Patrick Winston, one of the central figures in Artificial Intelligence. He will talk about MIT's Genesis story-understanding system and its many complex, varied aspects. Genesis reads *Macbeth...* This kind of project is what working with literature should really be about! ⌣

The afternoon invited speaker is a poet and a scholar, a strong voice in Digital Poetics, Loss Pequeño Glazier from SUNY Buffalo. He will tell us about poetic expression in array spaces of computational constellation, and illustrate it with his own take on Robin Blaser's influential "The Moth Poem".

There are seven regular papers on a variety of exciting topics, some of which have never been discussed at this workshop. Moshe Koppel, Moty Michaely and Alex Tall tell us about reconstructing the most original form of ancient manuscripts when multiple copies are available. Angel Daza, Hiram Calvo and Jesús Figueroa-Nazuno present their work on generating stories that are characterized by literary style. An intriguing paper by Xanda Schofield and Leo Mehr analyzes stereotypical gender roles using a corpus of film scripts.

Poetry, as always, figures strongly at the workshop. Arya Rahgozar and Diana Inkpen discuss ways in which one can distinguish automatically the periods in the Persian poet Hafez's life when he wrote his ghazals. Alex Estes and Christopher Hench take us on a brief tour of Middle High German epic poetry: how a Conditional Random Field model can automatically annotate meter in such poems.

Andrea Gagliano, Emily Paul, Kyle Booten and Marti Hearst look at figurative speech, a frequent guest in poetry. They show how continuous word vectors, a new promising technique, help generate interesting figure-of-speech relationships.

---

[1] https://sites.google.com/site/clfl2016/ – there are links to the Web sites for the previous workshops.
[2] http://csli-lilt.stanford.edu/

Marie Dubremetz and Joakim Nivre present another chapter of their work on detecting the rhetorical phenomenon of *chiasmus* in text.

All papers will be presented orally. Some of the authors will also put up posters. You can look at them during the day, and perhaps talk to the authors during the breaks.

There will be one new element at this year's workshop: a software demo. Olga Scrivner from Indiana University will show her team's Interactive Text Mining Suite, meant to visualize data for literary studies. She will also present a brief teaser right after lunch.

Well, that is it, more or less. Without further ado, let us invite you to enjoy this volume. We expect to see you in San Diego! ☺

Anna Feldman, Anna Kazantseva and Stan Szpakowicz

Patrick Henry Winston (http://people.csail.mit.edu/phw/)

Short bio

A graduate of MIT, Patrick Winston is Ford Professor of Artificial Intelligence and MacVicar Faculty Fellow at the Massachusetts Institute of Technology. His Genesis research group focuses on developing a computational account of human intelligence and how it differs from that of other species, with special attention to modeling human story telling and comprehension. Author and editor of numerous books, including *Artificial Intelligence*, he served as Director of the MIT Artificial intelligence Laboratory (now part of MIT's CSAIL Laboratory) for 25 years. He is now Research Coordinator for the multi-university, multi-disciplinary Center for Brains, Minds, and Machines centered at MIT.

Invited talk: *Genesis Reads Macbeth: The Role of Stories in Human Intelligence*

Abstract

I believe that human story competence—understanding, telling, authoring—lies at the center of human intelligence. To better understand that competence, my students and I are building the Genesis story-understanding system, a system that reads 100-sentence stories adapted from sources such as *Hansel and Gretel*, Crow creation myths, and Shakespeare's plays. I explain how our work has been guided by computational imperatives and challenged by our determination to model aspects of conceptual understanding, cultural bias, hypothetical reflection, personality modeling, listener-aware telling, on demand authoring, mental illness, and concept-based summary and search. I conclude with speculations on whether Genesis can really understand literature without a body, relating the question to the metaphor of the cave in Plato's Republic.

Loss Pequeño Glazier (http://epc.buffalo.edu/authors/glazier/)

Short bio

Dr. Loss Pequeño Glazier is Director of the Electronic Poetry Center/E-Poetry Festivals and Professor, Department of Media Study, SUNY Buffalo. The EPC is the world's largest digital resource for innovative and digital poetry. Glazier is the author of two books-in-progress as well as Digital Poetics: The Making of E-Poetries (Univ. of Alabama Press, 2002), *Anatman, Pumpkin Seed, Algorithm* (Salt Publishing, 2003), *Small Press: An Annotated Guide* (Greenwood, 1992), and hundreds of poems, essays, film, visual art, sound and digital works, as well as projects for dance, music, installations, and performance, including at the Neuberger Museum (SUNY Purchase), Royal Festival Hall (London), Instituto del Libro (La Habana), Guggenheim Museum (New York), UCLA Hammer Museum, Kulturforum Potsdamer Platz (Berlin), University of London, Le Divan du Monde (Paris), Bowery Poetry Club (New York), Brown University, and the Palazzo delle Arti Napoli. Glazier's work in digital writing focuses on code and its discontents, whether in natural language permutation, translation, computer programming, computational linguistics and aesthetic, spatial, and poetics. His author page contains numerous examples of his work.

Invited talk: *"The Not-Moth": Poetic Expression in Array Spaces of Computational Constellation*

Abstract

My talk provides an introduction to what I call "array poetics": using computer-generated groupings of natural language strings to explore new resonances of poetic space. To explore this space, I describe "The Not-Moth", my own digital poem written as a response to, and reflection on, Robin Blaser's "The Moth Poem", an early, influential poem in the San Francisco Renaissance of the 1960s. I investigate the dynamics, edition particulars, and the poetics of Blaser's original poem sequence. Then I think about how the qualities of this influential early work might be cast using the tools of today's technology – not to re-write the poem, but to respond to it through a computer-media composition reflecting some of its forms and language framings, while adding my own digital insights to the undertaking. To this end, the techniques he explored, innovative at the time, are viewed through my lens of "array poetics", the extension of nuances of textual variance through the computer manipulation of poetic language. In my talk, I give an overview of array poetics, including a non-technical explanation of "strings" (individual lines of natural language poetry), the "array" (groupings of such lines), and their arrangement ("coding") in exploring the possibilities of variant phrasing in expressive electronic language. Looking at the "array", I also suggest the implications of the "space between" strings, in the same way one might glimpse the "space between" lines of printed poetry, but here expanded in nuance through the basic digital frameworks (HTML, CSS, and select open-source tools) available in New Media writing. Ultimately the aim is, through technology – as well despite technology – to produce literary language in New Media in its full richness and expressive depth.

Program Committee

Apoorv Agarwal (Columbia University)
Cecilia Ovesdotter Alm (Rochester Institute of Technology)
Sandy Baldwin (Rochester Institute of Technology)
David Bamman (Carnegie Melon University)
Peter Boot (Huygens Institute for Netherlands History)
Chris Brew (Thomson-Reuters)
Julian Brooke (University of Toronto)
Micha Elsner (Ohio State University)
David Elson (Google)
Mark Finlayson (MIT)
Pablo Gervás Gómez-Navarro (Universidad Complutense de Madrid)
Roxana Girju (University of Illinois at Urbana-Champaign)
Amit Goyal (University of Maryland)
Graeme Hirst (University of Toronto)
Matthew Jockers (University of Nebraska–Lincoln)
Justine Kao (Stanford University)
Mike Kestemont (University of Antwerp)
Rada Mihalcea (University of Michigan)
David Mimno (Cornell University)
Saif Mohammad (National Research Council Canada)
Nick Montfort (Massachusetts Institute of Technology)
Sebastian Padó (Universität Stuttgart)
Livia Polanyi (LDM Associates)
Owen Rambow (Columbia University)
Caroline Sporleder (Georg-August-Universität Göttingen)
Reid Swanson (University of California, Santa Cruz)
Rob Voigt (Stanford University)
Marilyn Walker (University of California, Santa Cruz)
Bei Yu (Syracuse University)

Invited Speakers

Patrick Henry Winston, Massachusetts Institute of Technology
Loss Pequeño Glazier (State University of New York at Buffalo)

Organizers

Anna Feldman (Montclair State University)
Anna Kazantseva (National Research Council of Canada)
Stan Szpakowicz (University of Ottawa)

Table of Contents

Conference Program

Thursday, June 16, 2016

Session I

9:00–9:05 Welcome

9:05–10:00 *Genesis reads Macbeth: The role of stories in human intelligence* (invited talk)
Patrick Henry Winston

10:00–10:30 *Supervised Machine Learning for Hybrid Meter*
Alex Estes and Christopher Hench

Coffee break

Session II

11:00–11:30 *Automatic Text Generation by Learning from Literary Structures*
Angel Daza, Hiram Calvo and Jesús Figueroa-Nazuno

11:30–12:00 *Intersecting Word Vectors to Take Figurative Language to New Heights*
Andrea Gagliano, Emily Paul, Kyle Booten and Marti A. Hearst

12:00–12:30 *Gender-Distinguishing Features in Film Dialogue*
Alexandra Schofield and Leo Mehr

Supervised Machine Learning for Hybrid Meter

Alex Estes & Christopher Hench
University of California, Berkeley
Department of German
Berkeley, CA 94720, USA
{estes,chench}@berkeley.edu

Abstract

Following classical antiquity, European poetic meter was complicated by traditions negotiating between the prosodic stress of vernacular dialects and a classical system based on syllable length. Middle High German (MHG) epic poetry found a solution in a hybrid qualitative and quantitative meter. We develop a CRF model to predict the metrical values of syllables in MHG epic verse, achieving an F-score of .894 on 10-fold cross-validated development data (outperforming several baselines) and .904 on held-out testing data. The method used in this paper presents itself as a viable option for other literary traditions, and as a tool for subsequent genre or author analysis.

1 Introduction

The divergence of Latin into distinct regional dialects had profound linguistic and literary implications for all of Europe. Even before the Middle Ages, the syllable length of classical Latin had been nearly forgotten in the vernacular.[1] Latin poetry had used quantitative meter, whereby syllable length was the organizing principle. However, the emerging dialects differed from Latin in that stress became a phonologically important feature, and so-called qualitative meter predominated. In order to reconcile these linguistic differences, poetic forms emerged in which meter relied on both stress and syllable length. These hybrid metrical forms pose unique challenges to automated scansion (the process of determining the metrical value of each syllable for a line of poetry). In applying machine learning techniques to scan syllables of a hybrid meter, we believe we can contribute to the study of both metrics and poetics, medieval and otherwise. Our system serves not only pedagogical purposes by introducing students to the meter of medieval German epic poetry, but also presents itself as a tool for further research in author identification or topic modeling metrical form.

To illustrate quantitative meter, we consider the epic poetry of Latin and Greek. Each line consists of six feet, each foot typically a dactyl (a long syllable followed by two short syllables) or spondee (two long syllables). A syllable is considered long if it has a long vowel or diphthong, or ends in a consonant (Hayes, 1989). All other syllables are short. The first line of Virgil's *Aeneid* serves as example:[2]

ārma vi|rumque ca|nō, Tro|jae qui|prīmus ab|ōris
— ◡◡ | — ◡ ◡|— —|— — —|— ◡ ◡|— —

Shakespeare's verse, on the other hand, exhibits qualitative meter, structured in iambic pentameter, where each line has five iambs (a bisyllabic foot consisting of an unstressed first syllable followed by a stressed second syllable). The first line of *Romeo and Juliet* is scanned below:[3]

|Two house|holds, both |alike |in dig|nity.|
| × ́× | × ́× |× ́× |× ́× |× ́×|

2 Middle High German Meter

This paper considers the meter of twelfth and thirteenth century Middle High German (MHG) epic

---

[1] Augustine writes toward the end of the fourth century that while he recognizes time intervals, he can no longer distinguish between long and short syllables: *syllabarum longarum et brevium cognicionem me non habere...* "I cannot recognize long and short syllables..." cf. Augustinus, *De musica*, III, 3, 5.

[2] — represents a long syllable and ◡ a short syllable.

[3] Every syllable is marked with × . The acute accent ́ marks stress.

1

Proceedings of the Fifth Workshop on Computational Linguistics for Literature, NAACL-HLT 2016, pages 1–8,
San Diego, California, June 1, 2016. ©2016 Association for Computational Linguistics

verse. Although written in a Germanic language, MHG poetry was greatly influenced by the Romance tradition. This heritage is evident in its hybrid metrical structure: MHG verse patterns according to both syllable stress and length (Bostock, 1947).

The predominating pattern is an alternation between stressed and unstressed syllables (Tervooren, 1997).[4] MHG epic verse employs trochaic tetrameter: each line has four feet (Bostock, 1947), and each foot is a trochee. Phonologically, a trochee consists of two syllables; the first syllable is stressed, and the second is unstressed. For example, the English word "better" is a trochee, but the word "alive" is not. The famous Longfellow epic poem *The Song of Hiawatha* is written in trochaic tetrameter, and the first line serves to illustrate this rhythm:

Should you ask me, whence these stories?
| x́   x | x́ x | x́   x | x́ x |

Similarly, the typical MHG epic verse foot is two syllables in length, a stressed syllable followed by an unstressed syllable. However, feet can also be filled by one or three syllables (Domanowski et al., 2009). If a foot is filled by one syllable, the syllable must be phonologically long. If the foot is filled by three syllables, either the first two or the last two syllables must both be phonologically short.

It is in these atypical feet that the influence of quantitative meter, where syllable length is the key factor, becomes evident. We must slightly redefine the foot to account for this. Syllable length is measured in morae. Phonologically, a mora is a unit of time such that a short syllable has one mora and a long syllable has two morae (Fox, 2000).[5] A foot in this meter is more precisely defined as having two morae, not necessarily two syllables.[6] Indeed, the mora, not the syllable, has been called the fundamental unit of MHG verse (Tervooren, 1997, p. 1), although the mora functions differently in this po-

etic tradition than in its phonological definition. If a foot has only one syllable, the syllable must be long because a long syllable is two morae and the MHG foot requires two morae. A short syllable cannot be the only syllable in a foot, since it cannot be two morae. If a foot has three syllables, two must be short because only short syllables can be scanned as half morae, together forming one mora.[7] The other syllable is analyzed as one mora, yielding the required two morae in the foot. To summarize, a syllable can have one of three length values: mora, half mora, or double mora. A half mora must be phonologically short, and a double mora must be phonologically long. Phonological length is otherwise irrelevant and any syllable can be one mora.

In addition to length, as a function of morae, syllables are also assigned stress. There are three stress values: primary, secondary, or unstressed. Primary stress is assigned to the first or only stressed syllable in a word. Secondary stress is assigned to any following stressed syllable(s) in that word. All other syllables are unstressed.[8]

The final mora of the final foot of a line is omitted by convention. This is construed as a pause, and receives its own symbol in the scansion, even though there is no corresponding word or syllable. A short, word final syllable may also be elided before a word beginning with a vowel. MHG epic verse permits up to three syllables in anacrusis (a series of syllables at the beginning of a line that do not count in the meter). These syllables may or may not carry lexical or syntactic stress, but they are always scanned as unstressed morae.

The above features yield eight possible metrical values for any syllable:

---

[4]There is no consensus view on MHG meter. For this work we have most closely followed the viewpoints presented by Domanowski et al. (2009) and Heusler (1956), as well as more explicitly addressed the function of morae.

[5]For example, the English word "red" has two morae since it ends in a consonant, whereas the first syllable in the English word "reduce" has one mora, since it ends in a short vowel.

[6]It can be helpful to think of MHG meter in the musical sense. Each foot is a measure of 2/4 meter, where one mora is equivalent to one quarter note (Bögl, 2006).

[7]Occasionally very weakly stressed long syllables can also count as a half mora.

[8]The metrical distinction between different degrees of stress is rooted in phonological reality (Giegerich, 1985): in a word with many syllables, one syllable usually has a primary stress, and the others have either secondary or weak stress. For example, many pronounce the English word "anecdotal" with secondary stress on the first syllable, primary stress on the third syllable, and weakest stress on the second and fourth syllables.

- **mora - primary stress** (×́): a syllable with primary stress

- **mora - secondary stress** (×̀): a syllable with secondary stress

- **mora - unstressed** (×): an unstressed syllable

- **half mora - primary stress** (◡́): a short syllable with primary stress; according to metrical convention the preceding syllable must be long

- **half mora - secondary stress** (◡̀): a short syllable with secondary stress

- **half mora - unstressed** (◡): a short unstressed syllable

- **double mora** (—): a stressed long syllable; double morae always carry primary stress

- **elision** (ẹ): an elided syllable

Line 1 of Hartmann von Aue's *Der arme Heinrich* is prototypical. Each foot consists of a stressed syllable followed by an unstressed syllable. There is a one-syllable anacrusis:[9]

Ein | rîter | sô ge|lêret | was[10]
× | ×́ × | ×́ ×|×́ × | ×́ ^

Line 6 also begins with one syllable in anacrusis. The second foot has a stressed mora consisting of two syllables, each one a half mora. The third foot has one syllable; a diphthong allows it to be scanned as long. The final foot has a mora with secondary stress, since the preceding syllable is stressed and in the same word:

der |nam im |manege |schou|we[11]
× | ×́   × | ◡́ ◡ × | — | ×̀ ^

Line 34 has no anacrusis, and in the second foot two half mora syllables form the unstressed mora:

|die ein |ritter in |sîner |jugent[12]
| ×́   × |×́ ◡ ◡ |×́ × | ◡́ ◡ ^

Line 8 shows an elided syllable in the second foot:

dar |an be|gundẹ er |suo|chen[13]
× |×́ × | ×́   × | — | ×̀ ^

---

[9] ^ represents the rest for the empty mora at the end of a line. Note that this notation differs slightly from that which is used for classical and Shakespearian verse.

[10]"There was a knight so learned"

[11]"he looked extensively,"

[12]"which a knight [should have] in his youth."

[13]"in [these books] he began to search,"

3 Previous Computational Approaches to Meter

There are two prevailing treatments of meter in the literature concerned with computational poetic text analysis. One approach takes a known meter and assigns syllables to stress patterns based on such parameters (Hartman, 1996). The second approach assumes nothing of the meter, and seeks to determine it by marking syllables and identifying patterns (Plamondon, 2006; McAleese, 2007; Greene et al., 2010; Agirrezabal et al., 2013; Navarro, 2015). Our approach draws more on the latter.

Previous scholarship has focused on relatively simple systems of meter and adopted rule-based, statistical, or unsupervised approaches. The hybrid nature of MHG meter, and other complex systems developing out of classical antiquity, makes it difficult to scan poetry using these methodologies.[14]

4 Data

As supervised machine learning is a novel approach to scansion, annotated metrical data do not exist for MHG or most other languages. Following the scansion categorization system outlined above, the authors annotated syllables of MHG epic poetry into the eight categories of metrical value.

The annotated data consist of 450 lines from Hartmann von Aue's *Der arme Heinrich*, 200 lines from Wolfram von Eschenbach's *Parzival*, and 100 lines from Wirnt von Grafenberg's *Wigalois*.[15] An additional 10% (75 lines of Hartmann von Aue's *Iwein*) was annotated to be held-out for testing, yielding a total of 825 annotated lines. Summary statistics for all annotated data are given in Table 1.

Syllabification was performed prior to annotation. The principles of onset maximization (early formulation in Vennemann (1972)) and sonority sequencing (early formulation in Jesperson (1904)) govern syllabification in many languages, including, to a great degree, MHG. The division of words

---

[14]A strictly rule-based approach was undertaken by Friedrich Dimpel (2004). While Dimpel's approach is accurate, it is an arduous task, restrictive, and extremely language specific. Moreover, by identifying only the stressed syllables, it does not encompass the full complexity of MHG meter.

[15]Incorporating different poems from different poets accommodates varying styles of writing, but it also introduces more variability, an issue to be addressed in subsequent work.

	mean	std.	min.	max.
char. per line	21.34	3.39	9	32
syll. per line.	7.62	1.04	5	11
words per line	5.01	1.13	1	8
char. per word	4.26	1.96	1	17
syll. per word	1.52	.71	1	7
char. per syll.	2.80	.81	1	7

Table 1: Summary statistics for annotated dataset

with only one intervocalic consonant such as *ta-ge* "days" poses no difficulties. Only certain consonant clusters necessitate further information from MHG phonology. For example, the orthographic sequence of a nasal followed by a velar obstruent, although representing simply a velar nasal in modern German, were in fact still two separate phonemes in MHG (Paul et al., 1982). Thus the word *lange* "long" is syllabified as *lan-ge*. Intervocalic affricates can be viewed as either ambisyllabic or biphonemic, for example in *sitzen* "sit"; under both interpretations the first syllable has a coda and the second has an onset. There are also instances where morpheme boundaries interfere with the otherwise normal processes of syllabification. For example, the common MHG suffix *-lich* in *wîplich* "female" results in the syllabification *wîp-lich*, not *wî-plich*, despite onset maximization preferring the latter. Accounting for these idiosyncrasies, beyond onset maximization and sonority sequencing, with additional rules resulted in syllabification with an accuracy of 99.4% on the first 1,000 words in Hartmann von Aue's *Iwein*, yielding a 95% confidence interval of 98.9% to 99.9%.

Annotation was carried out by both authors, who are trained in MHG scansion.[16] In the case that a line exhibits multiple permissible scansions, priority is given to the scansion which best preserves the alternation of stressed and unstressed syllables. If a decision still cannot be made, then stress is given to semantic importance. An additional consideration is the syntactic stress of a particular line. Clearly, such evaluations allow some room for interpretation. Nevertheless, on a sample of 100 lines from the annotated data (739 syllables), the Cohen's kappa co-

---

	Annotator 2							
	×	×́	×̀	—	◡	◡́	ẹ	◡̀
× (Annotator 1)	285	4	0	1	3	0	0	0
×́	0	225	1	0	1	0	0	0
×̀	1	2	74	0	2	0	0	0
—	1	2	0	72	0	0	0	0
◡	1	0	0	0	36	0	0	0
◡́	0	1	0	0	0	17	0	0
ẹ	0	0	0	0	0	0	9	0
◡̀	0	0	0	0	0	0	0	1

Table 2: Inter-annotator agreement confusion matrix

efficient for the inter-annotator agreement is .962. The greatest disagreement for the human annotators was among unstressed and stressed morae, and between unstressed morae and unstressed half morae (Table 2), implying both some stress and some value disagreement.

5 Conditional Random Fields Model

Our efforts were focused on constructing a Conditional Random Fields (CRF) model to predict scansion for MHG meter (Lafferty et al., 2001).[17] Features are applied to the focal syllable, as well as to the ten preceding syllables and the ten following syllables of the line, if present.[18] Our resulting MHG features and their motivations are:

- **Position within line**: the last mora of a line is always stressed, and double morae occur most often in the third foot.

- **Length of syllable in characters**: longer syllables are more likely to be stressed. Unstressed prefixes and suffixes tend to be maximally three characters.

- **Syllable characters**: the characters in a syllable can help identify grammatical morphemes that are often unstressed. Slices were taken of the first character, first and second characters, last three characters, last two characters, and last character.

- **Elision**: the last two characters of the previous syllable and the first two characters of the cur-

---

rent syllable are identified to detect conditions for elision.

- **Syllable weight and length**: syllables ending in a vowel or consonant are open and closed, respectively. Syllables ending in a short vowel are short; otherwise they are long. Such values are useful in identifying double or half mora syllables, which must be long or short respectively. For example, the syllable "schou" in line 6 of *Der Arme Heinrich* above is a double mora, and is accordingly long.

- **Word boundaries**: stress usually occurs on the first syllable of a word.

The model was tuned only on the development data and the best performing model was chosen. The resulting best model uses an L1 coefficient of 1.3 and L2 coefficient of .001. No further changes were made after the model features and parameters were selected.

6 Results and Comparison to Other Models[19]

To evaluate the performance of our CRF model, we compare against two baselines: an n-gram model cascading into regular expressions, and a Brill transformation-based model on top of the n-gram model, both using syllables as units, just as the CRF model does. The n-gram model consists of cascading trigram, bigram, unigram, and regular expressions models, i.e. first a label is predicted based on the previous two labels, if possible; otherwise it is predicted based on the previous one label, and if the first two models fail it is predicted solely based on the label probability for the syllable itself. If the syllable did not appear in the training data, and it cannot be predicted by the first three models, it resorts to regular expressions. Based on MHG scansion theory and observations while annotating, syllables with long vowels were assigned to double mora, short syllables to unstressed mora, and the remaining syllables to mora with primary stress (which proved important to recognize stress alternation). The n-gram model was implemented with default settings.

---

[19]The results for all models are 10-fold cross-validated.

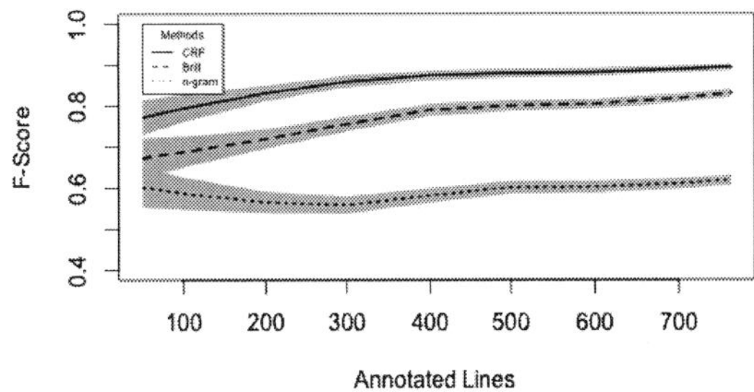

Figure 1: F-score of different models with 95% confidence intervals

The Brill model (Brill, 1995), implemented with the help of NLTK (Bird et al., 2009), first assigns the most likely label from the n-gram model described above, and then generates rules to improve the initial estimate of the n-gram model according to the training data. It then iterates over these rules, correcting labels until accuracy no longer increases. The Brill model was implemented with a maximum of 200 rules.

The n-gram model found little success even with added training data, ending with an accuracy of only 61.8%. The transformation-based Brill model improved quickly upon the n-gram model, but plateaued at 82.8% accuracy. Figure 1 shows the increase in accuracy with an increase in the number of annotated lines for all models, suggesting that marginal returns to annotation begin to diminish significantly after around 400 lines, or, in the case of MHG, about 3,000 syllables. Supervised machine learning thus proves to be an economical option for languages with complex meter.

The final results of the cross-validated CRF model are given in Table 3 in descending order of frequency in the data, along with a final held-out test set of 75 lines from Hartmann von Aue's *Iwein*. The model achieves an F-score of .894 on the cross-validated development data and .904 on the held-out testing data.

Apart from the infrequent half morae with secondary stress and elisions, the confusion matrix highlights four other problematic situations: (1) stressed morae marked as unstressed morae, (2) unstressed morae marked as stressed morae, (3) dou-

| | held-out | | | |
metrical value	F	obs.	F	obs.
mora - unstr.	.922	2403	.938	253
mora - prim.	.918	2025	.947	216
mora - sec.	.856	437	.880	37
double mora	.842	425	.865	34
half mora - unstr.	.574	231	.585	41
half mora - prim.	.771	103	.737	11
elision	.763	65	.500	2
half mora - sec.	0	4	0	0
(macro) average	.894		.904	

Table 3: CRF model F-score for individual metrical values and (macro) average in development and on held-out data

CRF	Brill
(1) not x́ if next syll. is end of line	(1) x́ → × if at word boundary and following syll. is x́
(2) — if end of line is next syll.	(2) x́ → — if followed by x̀ and word boundary
(3) ẹ if last char is "e" and first char. of next syll. is "e"	(3) × → x̀ if end of line
(4) not — if syll. is open and light	(4) x̀ → x́ if monosyllabic
(5) × if syll in pos. +7 is not end of line	(5) × → x́ if following syll. is "ge"

Table 4: Top five CRF features and Brill rules

ble morae marked as unstressed morae, and (4) unstressed half morae marked as unstressed morae. Three of these issues mirror those of the human annotators. Issues (1) and (2) are attributable not only to the frequency with which these features appear, but also to the pattern of alternating stress. If the stress assignment on one syllable is wrong, then it will likely be wrong for all following syllables in the line. (1) and (2) also affect (3), as shown below in line 14 of *Der arme Heinrich*, where the CRF model labels the penultimate syllable as an unstressed mora, when a double mora is correct:

und dâ mitẹ er sich möhte[20]

CRF model: | x́ × | x́ × | x́ × | x̀ ^
correct: × | x́ × | x́ × | — | x̀ ^

This error can be attributed to the overgeneralization of stress alternation. Formally, the model's prediction constitutes a metrically valid line of verse, but it cannot be correct for this particular line because the first syllable in *möhte* must be stressed. The model notably identifies the elision correctly. The worst performance, on unstressed half morae (4), paints a different picture, as illustrated in 21,7 of *Parzival*:

unsern goten, die in uns brâhten[21]

CRF model: × × | x́ × × | x́ × | — | x̀ ^
correct: × × | x́ ˘ ˘ | x́ × | — | x̀ ^

The model correctly predicts stress, but does not hold to the constraints of a foot as defined above. While these errors may be common, they are not as severe as the situation depicted in the first example.

The top five highest scoring features of the CRF model and rules of the Brill model are given in Table 4. The CRF feature scores show that syllable quality is helpful (4), something the Brill model cannot generalize. Both models recognize alternation, but while the Brill model adopts a more general rule (1), CRF features (1) and (5) recognize alternation using the number of syllables and the end of the line. CRF feature (5) also accounts for anacrusis. Notably, the Brill model took more advantage of word boundaries in (1) and (2), while these features rank lower in the CRF model. Features for phonemes do not rank high individually, unsurprising considering their impact among the other features. Nevertheless, "ver" and "ge" (MHG prefixes) both score highly in the CRF for marking a syllable unstressed, but only "ge" ranks as a top five rule for the Brill model.

The scores from both models confirm extant MHG metrical theory and suggest new methods of approach for students of MHG meter. Instead of first marking stress, as suggested by *Minimalmetrik* (1997) and the pedagogically oriented website Mittelhochdeutsche Metrik Online (2009), it may be useful to first determine the cadence and anacrusis, as noted in CRF features (1), (2), (5), and Brill rule (3). The advantage of this approach is not mistakenly marking stress in anacrusis. Stress can then be marked in the remaining syllables, and metrical values can be assigned based on phonological features. These results and insights support our feature decisions and our implementation of a CRF model.

---

[20]"and with which he might"

[21]"to our gods, who brought him to us"

7 Conclusion

This paper has presented a new application of machine learning models to poetry, specifically to traditions with hybrid meter. It promises to contribute to other literary interests in computational linguistics such as author and genre analysis. Research has shown that a proper account of meter must consider its variation throughout an entire text (Golston, 2009); automated scansion makes this a realistic enterprise. In applying this method, researchers can survey large scale variation within and across texts to discover the patterns that characterize authors and genres. Indeed, subtle differences in meter may prove to be distinct authorial voice or reveal significant stylistic choices. This paper also paves the way for further work such as: cluster analysis of meter over a large corpus of texts, topic modeling cadence across genre, and charting the literary affect of meter.[22]

Acknowledgments

We are grateful to David Bamman for commenting on drafts, and to the anonymous reviewers for useful feedback. This work was generously supported by Digital Humanities at Berkeley.

---

[22]The data and source code for this paper are available online at https://github.com/henchc/CLFL_2016.

References

[Agirrezabal et al.2013] Manex Agirrezabal, Bertol Arrieta, Aitzol Astigarraga, and Mans Hulden. 2013. ZeuScansion: a tool for scansion of English poetry. *Finite State Methods and Natural Language Processing*, pages 18–24.

[Bird et al.2009] Steven Bird, Edward Loper, and Ewan Klein. 2009. *Natural Language Processing with Python*. O'Reilly Media Inc.

[Bögl2006] Herbert Bögl. 2006. *Abriss der mittelhochdeutschen Metrik: mit einem Übungsteil*. G. Olms, Hildesheim ; New York.

[Bostock1947] J. Knight Bostock. 1947. *Der Arme Heinrich by Hartman von Ouwe*. Basil Blackwell and Mott, Oxford.

[Brill1995] Eric Brill. 1995. Transformation-based error-driven learning and natural language processing: A case study in part-of-speech tagging. *Computational linguistics*, 21(4):543–565.

[Dimpel2004] Friedrich Dimpel. 2004. *Computergestützte textstatistische Untersuchungen an mittelhochdeutschen Texten - Bd. II. Daten und Programme*. A. Francke, Tübingen.

[Domanowski et al.2009] Anna Domanowski, Yochanan Rauert, Hanno Rüther, and Tomas Tomasek. 2009. Mittelhochdeutsche Metrik Online. https://www.uni-muenster.de/MhdMetrikOnline/. Accessed on 04-02-2016.

[Fox2000] Anthony Fox. 2000. *Prosodic Features and Prosodic Structure: The Phonology of Suprasegmentals*. Oxford University Press, New York.

[Giegerich1985] Heinz J. Giegerich. 1985. *Metrical Phonology and Phonological Structure: German and English*. Cambridge University Press, Cambridge.

[Golston2009] Chris Golston. 2009. Old English Feet. In *Versatility in Versification: Multidisciplinary Approaches to Metrics*, pages 105–122. Peter Lang.

[Greene et al.2010] Erica Greene, Tugba Bodrumlu, and Kevin Knight. 2010. Automatic analysis of rhythmic poetry with applications to generation and translation. In *Proceedings of the 2010 conference on empirical methods in natural language processing*, pages 524–533. Association for Computational Linguistics.

[Hartman1996] Charles O. Hartman. 1996. *Virtual Muse: Experiments in Computer Poetry*. Wesleyan University Press, Hanover, N.H.

[Hayes1989] Bruce Hayes. 1989. Compensatory Lengthening in Moraic Phonology. *Linguistic Inquiry*, 20:253–306.

[Jespersen1904] Otto Jespersen. 1904. *Lehrbuch der Phonetik*. Teubner, Leipzig.

[Lafferty et al.2001] John D. Lafferty, Andrew McCallum, and Fernando C. N. Pereira. 2001. Conditional

Random Fields: Probabilistic Models for Segmenting and Labeling Sequence Data. In *Proceedings of the Eighteenth International Conference on Machine Learning*, ICML '01, pages 282–289. Morgan Kaufmann Publishers Inc.

[Longfellow1932] Henry Wadsworth Longfellow. 1932. *The poems of Longfellow, including Evangeline, The song of Hiawatha, The courtship of Miles Standish, Tales of a wayside inn.* B. A. Cerf, D. S. Klopfer, New York.

[McAleese2007] Gareth McAleese. 2007. Improving Scansion with Syntax: an Investigation into the Effectiveness of a Syntactic Analysis of Poetry by Computer using Phonological Scansion Theory.

[Navarro2015] Borja Navarro. 2015. A computational linguistic approach to Spanish Golden Age Sonnets: metrical and semantic aspects. In *Proceedings of the Fourth Workshop on Computational Linguistics for Literature*, pages 105–113, Denver, Colorado, USA, June. Association for Computational Linguistics.

[Okazaki2007] Naoaki Okazaki. 2007. CRFsuite: a fast implementation of Conditional Random Fields (CRFs). http://www.chokkan.org/software/crfsuite/.

[Paul et al.1982] Hermann Paul, Hugo Moser, Ingeborg Schröbler, and Siegfried Grosse. 1982. *Mittelhochdeutsche Grammatik.* Max Niemeyer, Tübingen.

[Plamondon2006] M. R. Plamondon. 2006. Virtual Verse Analysis: Analysing Patterns in Poetry. *Literary and Linguistic Computing*, 21:127–141.

[Shakespeare and Gibbons1980] William Shakespeare and Brian Gibbons. 1980. *Romeo and Juliet.* The Arden edition of the works of William Shakespeare. Methuen, London ; New York.

[Tervooren1997] Helmut Tervooren. 1997. *Minimalmetrik zur Arbeit mit mittelhochdeutschen Texten.* Kümmerle Verlag, Göppingen.

[Vennemann1972] Theo Vennemann. 1972. On the Theory of Syllabic Phonology. *Linguistische Berichte*, 18:1–18.

[von Aue2004] Hartmann von Aue. 2004. *Der arme Heinrich.* Number 6 in Bibliothek des Mittelalters. Deutscher Klassiker Verlag.

[von Eschenbach et al.1994] Wolfram von Eschenbach, Karl Lachmann, Eberhard Nellmann, and Dieter Kuhn. 1994. *Parzival.* Bibliothek deutscher Klassiker. Deutscher Klassiker Verlag, Frankfurt am Main, 1 aufl edition.

[von Grafenberg2014] Wirnt von Grafenberg. 2014. *Wigalois: Text der Ausgabe von J.M.N. Kapteyn.* De Gruyter Texte. De Gruyter, Berlin, 2., überarb. aufl edition.

Automatic Text Generation by Learning from Literary Structures

Angel Daza & Hiram Calvo & Jesús Figueroa-Nazuno

Centro de Investigación en Computación, Instituto Politécnico Nacional, CIC-IPN

J. D. Bátiz e/ M. O. de Mendizábal, 07738, Mexico City, Mexico

{josdaza.a@gmail.com, hcalvo@cic.ipn.mx, jfn@cic.ipn.mx}

Abstract

Most of the work dealing with automatic story production is based on a generic architecture for text generation; however, the resulting stories still lack a style that can be called literary. We believe that in order to generate automatically stories that could be compared with those by human authors, a specific methodology for fiction text generation should be defined. We also believe that it is essential for a story to convey the effect of originality to the person who is reading it. Our methodology proposes corpus-based generation of stories that could be called creative and also have a style similar to human fiction texts. We also show how these stories have plausible syntax and coherence, and are perceived as interesting by human evaluators.

1 Introduction

Natural Language Generation (NLG) is the process of constructing natural language outputs from non-linguistic inputs: its task is to map meaning to text. The task of automatically generating human language has proved to be much more difficult than it had been expected. In general, concepts strongly tied to human intelligence, such as art, creativity and storytelling, are just beginning to be seriously explored with an automatic approach. That is because of the problems they trigger, such as dealing with meaning, intentionality, planning and common sense knowledge, just to mention a few.

In this work, we propose a new method of automatic generation of fiction text. We intend to achieve this by attempting a formalization of the creative writing process. Thus, we believe that we can define a simplified method of automating the process of creative writing. With such a method, we will be able to generate fiction texts that contain novel and coherent sentences by adapting them from previously seen fiction texts.

We think that current approaches do not attend to the fact that literature, unlike other kinds of texts such as news or business reports, does not aim to solely inform about raw facts on some information domain of the world. On the contrary, the primary intention of literary texts is to use language properties to describe events aesthetically, with a certain special *style*, and through these descriptions transform the way we perceive reality (Eco, 2005). So, what we call literary style is the act of producing meaning not just with content, but with the uses of language and text structure. A literary text is written to find new ways of expressing reality, and in general, to seek new meanings in language use. What we intend is not only to produce structured logical texts, but to create an architecture that can produce stories that pursue the imitation of the properties that acknowledged here as *literary*.

We can distinguish three main current approaches to story generation: problem-solving, story grammars and the corpus-based approach. All of them focus on adapting existing universal generation techniques to the formalization of storytelling. This means that they tackle automatic generation of text by implementing story structures as a planning task instead of a linguistic problem, leaving behind the fact that language in literature is used in a more strongly distinct way than in everyday life.

The problem-solving approach sees generation as a search task, where a path needs to be found between a starting point and a goal state, and tries to implement common AI techniques to attack this problem. Examples of this approach are in (Meehan, 1977; Swartjes and Theune, 2006; Pérez, 1999).

Proceedings of the Fifth Workshop on Computational Linguistics for Literature, NAACL-HLT 2016, pages 9–19,
San Diego, California, June 1, 2016. ©2016 Association for Computational Linguistics

The problem with that kind of work is that, while it tends to produce coherent stories, it also tends to be limited in the kind of stories generated, primarily because it mostly relies on hand-made factual databases.

Story grammars are also a common way to approach generation. It tries to formalize storytelling theory into generative grammars that produce text with a defined structure that can be called a story. Examples in this area are in (Thorndyke, 1977; Gervás, 2013). Like the problem-solving approach, the main weakness of story grammars is the high dependence on given information, in this case hand-made rules and predefined story-grammar structures.

More recently, the corpus-based approach has been used to eliminate human intervention – as much as possible – from the process of creating a story. The most successful work that follows this approach is (McIntyre and Lapata, 2009), where almost no human intervention is needed, but the results, while coherent, do not resemble a style that is easily recognizable as literary.

Here we present an example of a story produced by this approach:

The family has the baby. The baby is to seat the lady at the back. The baby sees the lady in the family. The family marries a lady for the triumph. The family quickly wishes the lady vanishes.

We consider it a non-literary text because it is formed by concatenating simple declarative sentences. This work clearly prioritizes the logical series of events and the existence of a clear narrative arc over text style. We, on the other hand, intend to prioritize a style that shows expressiveness and connects literary images in a new way. Only as a secondary goal do we intend to create a logical sequence of events. This happens to be not just a valid but a common approach in literature, especially from the last century.

Another corpus-based approach that has lately gained prestige because of its good results is the one based on Recurrent Neural Networks (RNN). Especially in the field of NLG, there is interesting work by Karpathy (2015), who trains character language models on RNN's and gets great results at the syntactic level of language. While we consider these re-sults very impressive, we believe that our approach goes beyond the syntax in language. Unlike this kind of work, it intends to find a bridge between syntax and semantics, trying to generate texts which hold both syntactic coherence and meaningful semantic relationships. Karpathy's work manages to generate syntactic style with high fidelity, but he does not give importance to the meaning of the produced text. Conversely, our task is to generate texts that, while maintaining correct syntax, also contain a narrative arc, where a reader could recognize a story.

The present work tries to generate original and novel texts based on a directed combinatorial perspective by exploiting syntactic and semantic patterns found in fiction stories that have already been written. We attempt to emulate human authors in the sense that we as authors do not produce a new text from a fresh start. Instead, we apply previous knowledge acquired from what we have already read and experienced.

One of the main contributions of this work is the bottom-up approach, where a single word is the starting point, and the meaning of the generated text *emerges* automatically together with linguistic production. Only in the end is a general structure given to the text in order to be able to present it as a story. We were strongly influenced by the NLG architecture presented in (Reiter and Dale, 2000), in that we reuse their concepts, but we try to emphasize text style instead of text planning.

Another important aspect that we explore in this work is creativity. As we let text meaning emerge instead of determining it from the beginning, the generation of stories can be called creative, since the text holds a series of meanings that are not necessarily present in the corpus. To prove this, we demonstrate how human evaluators consider our texts at least as creative as those which were written explicitly by a human author.

2   Literary Structures

We decided to propose a new kind of structures, which will be used as the building blocks of our text's sentences. We did this because canonical syntactic structures are not enough for our purpose of creating novel sentences without entirely losing semantic coherence. We propose five types of structures: Noun Phrases with Verb (NPV), Verb Phrases with Preposition (VPP), Previous Prepositional Phrases (PPP), Simple Phrases (PHR) and Clauses (CLS).

NPV: it is a Noun Phrase that act as an agent in a sentence, together with the action of that agent, the main verb. Examples of NPVs are: "The white-haired woman looked" and "The white-haired woman opened".

VPP: a Verb Phrase holds a verb with its respective complements. Usually, VPs have embedded Prepositional Phrases (which represent the circumstance of the specific action), so in order to detach more effectively the action from its context we propose the VPP structure which is the result of removing the prepositional phrase from the VPs. VPPs only keep verbs with their respective object and a preposition at the end, if it has one. For example, the VP "undertake the development and staffing of the world and its habitants" can be converted into the VPP "undertake the development of".

PPP: a Prepositional Phrase is the circumstance of a VP. For example, if we wish to put a preposition predicate to the VPP "stalked a dozen yards away beneath" the natural question would be "beneath what?" A possible answer could be "beneath the trees".

PHR: Literary texts tend to have subordinate clauses embedded in complex sentences. In order to avoid the complexity of long sentences, and also with the purpose of decontextualizing, we extract simple phrases, subordinates and coordinate phrases into a different literary structure named PHR, in order to be able to combine them also as separate ideas.

CLS: We give the name of special clauses to those clauses that hold an immediate cause-effect relation. Those relations can be found if the sentences containing one or more of the following keywords: so, because, if-then, when, therefore, consequently, hence, for the reason that, as a result, as a consequence.

2.1 Word-Clause Similarity Measure

We will use special clauses (CLS) in the generation step as our story endings. That is why we want to find semantic relatedness between the main word of a story and its possible endings. Hence, a separate database is kept for storing the semantic similarity between words and CLS's. This database contains the most frequent nouns, adjectives and verbs as the keys, and its values are the concatenation of the semantic similarity score, which we call *semsim*, between that word and every CLS that was found. This is obtained with the help of the JCN Similarity Measure (Jiang and Conrath, 1997). With this score, given a word, we can know which are the CLSs semantically closest to that word.

The JCN similarity measure is a semantic metric based on both corpus statistics and lexical taxonomy. It takes advantage of the hierarchical structure that already exists in WordNet (Fellbaum, 1998) and also computes the information content (IC), which is derived from the co-occurrence distribution of that word in a given corpus. The IC of a concept is computed as:

$$IC(c) = log^{-1} P(c) \qquad (1)$$

In order to avoid polysemy problems, the measure considers not words but particular senses of words (a *synset* in WordNet). The JCN similarity measure can be seen in fact as the inverse of the distance between two synsets, counting the edges linking two senses to their lowest common subsumer (*lcs*) or parent in the WordNet hierarchy and finally incorporating the IC as an important decision factor.

$$JCN_{sim} = \frac{1}{IC(syn_1) + IC(syn_2) - IC(lcs)} \qquad (2)$$

We cannot use this measure directly because it can only make comparisons between two senses of words with the same lexical category; so, in order to achieve a comparison between a word and a phrase, we sum the semantic similarity *semsim* (see Equation 4) between the main word W and each of the n words inside the clause whose lexical category matches that of the main word:

$$CLS_{sim} = \sum_{k=0}^{n} semsim(W, w_k) \qquad (3)$$

We use the operation *semsim* because JCN measure works with word senses instead of words. Since words have been detached from their original context, it is quite difficult to trace their sense back, so we propose to analyze the similarity among every sense of each pair of words and keep the highest score found (that means we keep the highest semantic similarity that two words can have). The operation *semsim* can be defined as:

$$semsim(w_1, w_2) =$$

$$argmax \left\{ \sum_{i=1}^{x} \sum_{j=1}^{y} jcn_{sim}(s_i, s_j) \right\} \qquad (4)$$

where x is the number of senses of w1, and y is the number of senses of w2.

2.2 Sentence Generation

We propose to construct novel sentences based on a simple pattern as shown in Figure 1.

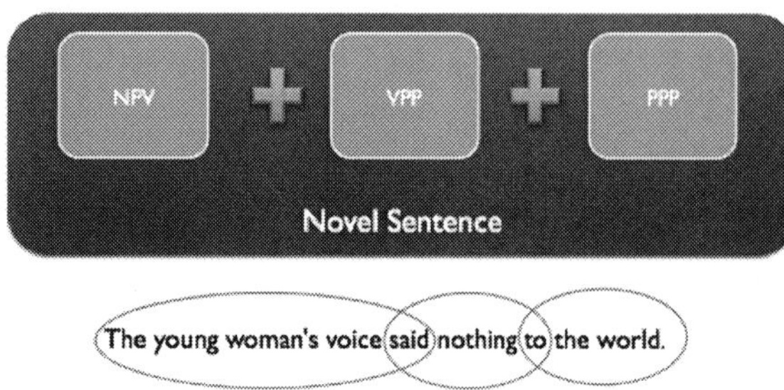

Figure 1: Novel sentences are intersected literary structures.

We can see that the proposed literary structures can be easily concatenated because of their intrinsic properties: An NPV always ends with a verb, a VPP always starts with a verb and ends with a preposition, and a PPP always starts with a preposition, so to construct a sentence, the algorithm just needs to find which of the structures intersect with each other. Given a word, we can have a large number of combinations among the connected phrases. We can start by choosing an NPV, and then look for all the VPPs that start with the same verb as the NPV's ending verb, and the same can be done with looking for the PPPs that start with the same preposition as the ending preposition of the chosen VPP. The next section will explain which structures are preferred and then how are they chosen.

The key idea is that, with this simple method, we can easily expand phrasal possibilities, starting from a main noun, into several different characters. Then, by looking at VPP intersections we can expand even more from the main verb into several predicates,

and finally, if we want a complex predicate, we expand the preposition into many prepositional complements.

2.3 Ranking Algorithm

We have said that a huge number of sentences can be built by freely combining all possible NPV+VPP+PPP structures. However, in order to get better syntactic coherence in our generated sentences, we defined a set of simple ranking rules for each of the three structures.

Each list of possible structures will be ordered according to a score that our ranking algorithm assigns to them. Every existing structure starts with a score of 1, and points will be added depending on the rules that we describe next. Finally, to retain the creative approach, we run the roulette wheel method in order to choose them. So, the higher-ranked structures will a better chance to be chosen, but each of them has a chance to be chosen anyway.

As an example, we show the set of rules that are followed to score NPV's (Table 1). It is important to mention that each structure follows a different set of rules to get scored, and we defined those rules based on writing manuals such as (Payne, 2011; Espinal et al., 2014; Pinker, 2014).

Feature	Score
NPV starts with *The*	+500
NPV starts with main word	+300
NPV starts with *A/an*	+300
NPV has one or more commas	+50
NPV has a subordinator	-100
NPV has the particle *to*	-300
NPV verbosity	+(Number of adjs*10)
NPV frequency	+(NPV freq*2)

Table 1: Ranking algorithm rules for NPV literary structures.

3 Proposed Architecture

Following the classical NLG process, previous story generation systems just add or remove capabilities to fulfill their specific goals. Besides, they strongly rely on handmade rules, knowledge bases, or schemes to overcome some of the linguistic problems that arise while generating text.

What we propose is to unify both text and story generation processes through a corpus-based approach, in order to get stories that produce the sensation of literary style instead of just a carefully planned and structured text. It still imitates NLG classic architecture components, but it uses them in a bottom-up way. Instead of generating language following a detailed document plan, we propose to start with a word as a basic unit (such as a verb, a noun or an adjective), and then let the story emerge based on the linguistic properties that this word holds in the knowledge base.

3.1 Corpus

Our algorithm was trained on a corpus of 9,560 books (which contained both short stories and complete novels) from around 1,100 different authors, which resulted in 1.6GB of text. It contains texts as antique as Homer's "Odyssey" and as present as George R. R. Martin's "Game of Thrones". The most frequent genre was science fiction: We have around 270 texts from Isaac Asimov, 170 from Douglas Adams, 110 from Arthur C. Clarke, for example. There is also classic literature – Honoré de Balzac (78 texts), Mark Twain (110 texts), Charles Dickens (54 texts) – and post-modern literature – 76 texts from William Burroughs and 12 from James Joyce, among many others.

As can be seen above, it is a heterogeneous corpus that covers a wide range of styles from different stages of the history of fiction texts. This allows the algorithm to learn from a wide range of styles, and because of this, our generator can produce texts in such a fashion that it is not easy to typecast it into a certain movement or known style.

The trained corpus resulted in more than 2 million processed sentences and more than 350,000 unique tokens (a single word could be converted into three tokens: the word-as-adjective, word-as-verb and word-as-noun was counted separately). We obtained approximately 7 million structures (3.3 million NPVs, 1.5 million VPPs, 1 million PPPs and PHRs and 60 thousand CLSs).

3.2 Knowledge Base Construction

We created a knowledge base by extracting existing relations of words and style from fiction texts – see Figure 2. We were looking for a mixture of texts that could produce text with a style not directly referable to any previously known story.

We separated sentences that are at most 100 words long, and also pragmatically neutral (sentences that do not express a question, a dialogue or quotation).[1] By using only pragmatically neutral sentences we can generalize (although there could be a few counterexamples) that the subject is the noun phrase or pronoun that immediately precedes the verb or auxiliary inside the sentence (Payne, 2011), which will help us in the story generation step. All these deletions, instead of limiting our information, help us to correctly detach even more phrases and isolate them from their original context.

As a first step, before constructing the database, we process the texts using Stanford Parser (Klein and Manning, 2003) in order to work with a set of parsed sentences instead of plain strings. Next, we identify the literary structures. After we have obtained the desired structures from the parsed corpus, we use the Named Entity Recognizer from the NLTK library (Bird et al., 2009) to extract proper names and entities found in text.[2] Then, we apply a ranking algorithm to every extracted structure, so every structure inside our knowledge base will have a score associated with it, in order to improve story coherence and avoid random choice at the generation step. At the same time, we index words and structures in such a fashion that given any word, we can automatically get all its associated structures. Likewise, given any structure index, we can immediately recover the specific list of words that form it. This will help our generation algorithm to navigate the knowledge base fast and also exploit possibilities of avoiding the generation of the same sentences repeatedly on each iteration. Lastly, we implemented our word-clause similarity measure to compute the closest structure for any given word.

We also introduced in the knowledge base a number of lists containing basic grammar details such as words that can receive a proper name, transitive verbs, English prepositions and pronouns. These are

---

[1]We do use the non-neutral sentences in the Special Clause Extraction, since those are already full sentences, thus they are not building blocks for creating new ones. They are the only sentences inserted in the generated text as they were found in the corpus, meaning that we can trust their syntax.

[2]We realize that the NER from NLTK is trained on news texts; however, we could not find an open library for recognizing entities in fiction texts.

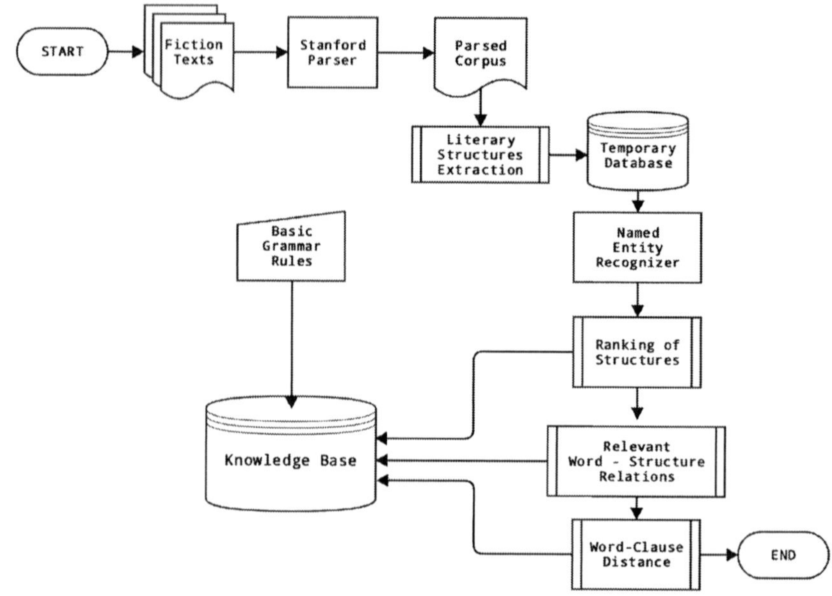

Figure 2: Knowledge Base construction diagram.

used to correct some of the mistakes that may arise while generating our sentences.

3.3 Text Generation Process

Once the knowledge base has been constructed, the first step for generating a story is to provide a word to the algorithm, so it can look for the literary structures that are directly connected to that word in our knowledge base. After extracting the needed structures, the algorithm reads and complements their rankings. Then, it proposes a new way to relate and combine them in order to generate novel sentences that will not only hold a literary style, but also will produce new meanings not necessarily present in the original sentences.

The proposed generator aims to maximize the impression of creativity, meaning that even if the content and quality of the produced sentences directly depend on the corpus, the sequence of sentences that make the output will not be easily traceable in the original sources. The algorithm will combine and modify as much as possible what is found in the knowledge base without losing coherence, producing a new piece of text in each iteration: an original story.

We should mention that we merged the modules of Surface Realization and micro-planning, doing

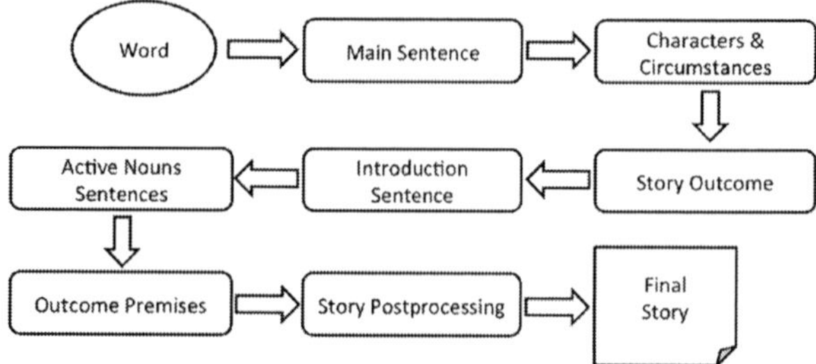

Figure 3: Overview of the text generation step.

both tasks in the same step. Style, content and language production will be managed as a whole, so creativity of the story will entirely be produced here. This way, we avoid being predictable while generating sentences of the same kind or of the same length for example. We also reduced the macro-planning task to a general schema that every story will follow. This was done in order to ensure that a story with a recognizable beginning and ending will always be created. We found that this was feasible without losing the creative approach because of the diversity of sentences that can be produced on the micro-planning step, which overshadow the macro structure of the final story.

4   Building a Story

We have established how we extract, classify and rank all the necessary building blocks for the generation step. We emphasize the importance of having a well-structured knowledge base for optimizing the text generation layer. In this section, we will mainly explain how the algorithm uses its knowledge base in order to construct a coherent story.

First, we will explain what we use as story macro-planning. It is nothing but a general template with fixed slots that will be filled, with the help of a few directives, at the end of the process. This template is filled step by step, and every step will be explained in detail together with the information that is tracked, for purposes of coherence, at the moment of generating a story. Before putting everything together, we make some grammar corrections (we mainly check verb conjugations, pronoun usage, NER substitutions and determine subjects of sentences for gender and number coherence inside sentences), which we call Story Post-processing. At last, we assemble everything together, and show the final output of the algorithm.

Main Sentence: It is not only the first step, but also the core of every story. Based on the input word, a novel sentence is constructed (NPV+VPP+ PPP). The main word will be considered as the main character of the story, and the other nouns that appear after the verb will be considered secondary characters.

Characters and Circumstances: In every step of text generation, we add to a small dictionary the different participants of the current plot (nouns) with their specific characteristics (adjectives), and the actions they have taken (verbs). By doing so, we avoid the presentation of the same character with contradictory adjectives (e.g., if we already said that a woman was young, we cannot refer to her as an old woman in later sentences). Also, if a noun has verbs attached to it, we know that it is an active noun in the story and can be considered an agent who can perform more actions in the future.

Story Outcome: Before elaborating more about our known characters and circumstances, we need to know at what outcome are we aiming at, in order to control a little more the semantics of our sentences. Thus, the next step is to look for a suitable story ending. We rely on our word-clause similarity measure to help us find a meaningful ending to our story. Once the main idea has been created, and based on the vocabulary that is present in it, the algorithm looks for the twenty closest clauses to the main idea. Once we have calculated the similarity of our main sentence to all the possible outcomes, we obtain the semantically ranked list of CLSs, and we choose the 20 top-ranked outcomes (the outcomes closest to our main sentence). Finally, the roulette method is applied to choose among the top-20 list what will become our story outcome.

Introduction Sentence: As we have said before, stories nowadays do not necessarily hold a classical structure of introduction, conflict and resolution. Even so, we believe that it is more intuitive for a reader to identify a text as a story if it begins in a classical manner. This is why we chose to have a few common story introductions, such as "Once upon a time", "There was once a", etc. This is added as a start in every story, so the reader immediately interprets every sentence as a part of some fiction text.

Active Noun Sentences: The algorithm will use simple phrases (PHRs) in order to go deeper into the characters of the story. At this step, we already have the introduction and the main idea of the story together with the story outcome. What is expected to appear next in a story is a little more information about the characters, so the algorithm looks for descriptions of the main word and the other words that appear to be active on the story. We consider a word as active if it is a noun and it has at least one verb (action) associated with it in our dictionary of characters and circumstances. In addition to the active nouns, the algorithm also looks for the noun that holds more connections (a connection is a link to a phrase that mentions the given word) in the knowledge base, in order to write another sentence about it (since it has many connections there should be plenty of things to say about it). The rest of active nouns may or may not be mentioned in more descriptive phrases. A random number is generated between zero and the number of active nouns, to determine how many more descriptive phrases will be included. This is done in order to avoid having a bunch of phrases mentioning diverse nouns and deviating too much from the main idea.

Outcome Premises: To advance the plot even

more, after we described the characters more, we have to look for a connection between the beginning of the story and the outcome. Based on a similar technique as character description, a separate entity dictionary is created for the outcome alone, and the algorithm now looks for the nouns that appear in the selected outcome, and tries to say more about them. The same as with character descriptions, we decided to avoid saying too much about nouns that deviate from the main plot. Consequently, again the algorithm produces a random number between zero and the number of nouns in the list, to choose which nouns will be described before the outcome.

Story Post-processing: The final sentences that will be part of the story have been already generated, but before assembling the story there are a few things to check. They mainly concern number and gender agreement between subjects and verbs, and between quantifiers and nouns, as well as the correct use of personal, possessive and relative pronouns. Also this step checks that all transitive verbs have an assigned complement, and all prepositions have a nominal phrase as a complement. This is done to avoid having truncated sentences and incomplete ideas. Finally, another important step here is the NER substitution to avoid situations when recognizable entities from other stories are mentioned in ours.

5   Story Example

Now that we have described our methodology to generate stories, we will proceed to show an actual example of the working of the algorithm. We start by generating a completely novel sentence, which will be our main sentence, by the formula NPV+VPP+PPP. The algorithm generates the following:

- NPV: *The first man, yawning, sleepy and bleary-eyed, the lazy beast, stumbled*
- VPP: *stumbled along*
- PPP: *along linguistic pathways that were something other than the most direct ones*

We show next the list of sentences that are concatenated to form a story.

1. **Introduction Sentence**:   Once upon a time there was a first man.

2. **Main Sentence**:   The first man, yawning, sleepy and bleary-eyed, the lazy beast, stumbled along linguistic pathways that were something other than the most direct ones.

3. **Main Character Name**: His name was Owen.

4. **Most Connected Entity Description**:   The great ones had gone to discuss high matters.

5. **Main Word Description**: Owen had brought shame to his door.

6. **Active Noun Descriptions**: The beast was not a showy beast, and it was rather small, having much of the blood.

7. **Outcome Premises**:   The fact that this poor simple mental retard couldn't make it work is beside the point. The only reason the person would be going into the water was to do something nasty with the nuclear mines, as the mundane world saw no great profit, commercial or artistic, to be reaped from our little field. A vague, unsatisfactory basis on which to risk the only life. The demon, steel strong and more than iron hard, leaped free to dispose of the men before him and around him. In somewhere, the rainforests of the people are being destroyed at an alarming rate by bulldozing and burning.

8. **Story Outcome**: It might have a real basis in fact, too, but the real reason is that we feel that a world with tigers and orangutans and rainforests and even small unobtrusive snails in it is a more healthy and interesting world for humans (and, of course, the tigers and orangutans and snails) and that a world without them would be dangerous territory.

We can observe a complete story, made out of structures that were extracted from different sources. Steps 1 and 3 work on templates automatically generated; Step 2 takes three structures (an NPV, a VPP and a PPP), each from a different source; Steps 4 and 5 are two PHRs; Step 6 is a single PHR; Step 7 is made of five concatenated PHRs, each one from a different source text; and finally, Step 8 is one of the 20 CLSs closest to the main word. Our story is then a complete text on its own, an original story, since it was made from 12 different pieces of text that were previously totally unrelated, but now tell a single narrative arc.

6 Experiments and Results

We evaluate the generated stories in a survey where people were asked to score different parameters in texts. Next, we will establish the aspects that are measured in the evaluation, and also the restrictions. Finally, we explain how the survey was applied to human evaluators and the obtained results.

Evaluators: The survey was successfully applied to a population of 32 individuals, all of them students. We considered it important to select individuals who had moderate to strong reading habits. We also kept track of gender (14 women and 18 men) and age balance (people were between 18 and 36 years old). Also the field of study of every evaluator was relevant. Evaluators came from heterogeneous fields such as the humanities (e.g., philosophy, linguistics, literature), engineering (e.g., biotechnology, computer, electronics), and sciences (e.g., cognitive neuroscience, math, chemistry). The complete population distribution by field of study is presented in Figure 4.

Field of Study

Figure 4: Evaluators' fields of study.

Story Selection: One of the biggest disadvantages of preserving the impression of creativity in the produced texts is this: We do not have entire control of the content and fluency of stories, so the algorithm does not always guarantee to produce a satisfactory text. We countervail this lack of hundred percent guarantee with the ability to produce several stories in short time (approximately five stories per minute). Since it is a new architecture, for now, we settled on producing several stories that could be analyzed by a human reader, who decides which one has achieved the algorithm's result expectations.

For the purpose of evaluation, we generated five instances of stories based on each of the thirty most frequent words (to give the algorithm a broader search space of structures), resulting on a total of 150 stories.[3] Three pre-evaluators read each story and selected those that contained fewer grammatical mistakes, had more lexical variation and a reasonable length. In the end, since we only needed to include four stories in our main survey, the four most voted stories were chosen.

6.1 Evaluation Survey

The survey is inspired by the Turing test, where people have to decide if the text they are reading was produced by another person or by an algorithm. The included texts are shown in Table 2, and judges were not informed about the origin of texts, so they could not know if it was an artificially generated text, or a text by a human author. Additionally, we decided to measure four more parameters: coherence, interest, originality and syntax quality.

Title	Author
Naked Lunch (fragment)	William Burroughs
A Big Man Existed	Machine
The Left Gets Threatened	Rachel Summer
The White Sky Met	Machine
A Beautiful Story	Machine
Finnegans Wake (fragment)	James Joyce
The First Man	Machine

Table 2: Texts that were presented to human judges

There are five questions for each text, and the evaluator can answer only by using a slider bar with two antonyms on the extremes, where she has to decide how close her opinion is to a given concept. The five questions consist each of a slider between two opposite concepts. The concepts evaluated were coherence, interest, originality and the quality of English. An evaluator is asked to give her preference towards a given concept. Each slider has a hidden value between 0.00 (the left most part of the slider) and 10.00 (the right most part of the slider), and it starts with the default neutral value of 5.00.

---

[3]Please refer to http://ebard.likufanele.com for more examples of generated stories

17

6.2 Results

We split our survey results in two, that is, we evaluated separately the scores given to human texts and the scores given to artificial texts. As shown in Figure 5, our texts obtained even more positive votes than the human texts. This shows that the evaluators were unable to identify directly any trace of artificiality in our generated texts. On the contrary, they even considered our texts to be more coherent, interesting and with acceptable syntax.

We chose to compare our texts with post-modern authors, because we wanted to emphasize that our texts were at least as experimental as the texts of those authors. This also opens the debate on the characteristics that normally people look for in order to explore outputs generated artificially. The fact that the evaluators scored our texts better than human texts only highlights the fact that people consider an output to be more *human* if they find it more familiar. Since our texts were less elaborate than human texts, evaluators got confused and tried to stick to the more familiar outputs, which happened to be our texts. This makes sense, since our generated texts are only combinations of other ordinary texts. In the end, this successfully proves that our artificial outputs were not recognizable among other literature works.

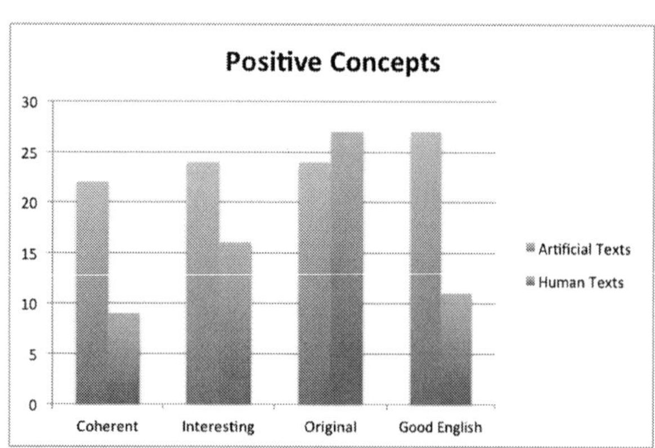

Figure 5: Votes received for positive concepts of each aspect.

To stress even more the creativity (Figure 6) perceived in our texts, we include a more detailed graph showing the percentage of votes that human and artificial texts obtained in each originality interval (we divided the slider in ten intervals to measure this). Recall that the intervals closer to zero mean originality and those closer to ten mean that the texts are common.

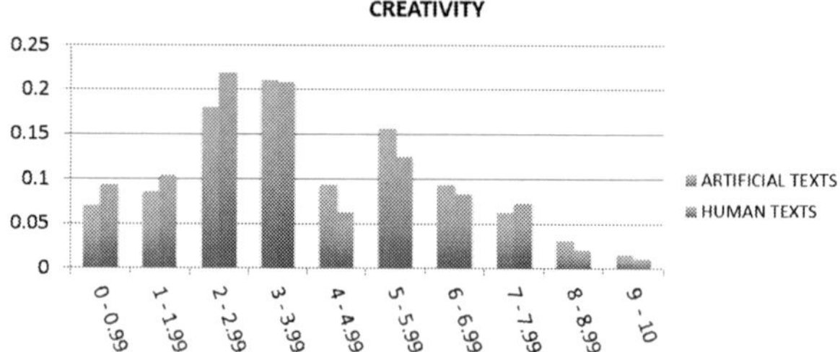

Figure 6: Percentage of votes obtained in the creativity aspect of texts.

There still is one more general chart that shows the overall semantic differential. This is an attempt to measure concept meanings by asking the judge where her position towards two opposite adjectives lie (Osgood et al., 1957). In this case we measured the judges' overall perception of texts. This chart (Figure 7) shows the semantic categorization of our generated texts, concluding that in general our texts were taken with a positive judgment. We included in the same chart the semantic differential of human texts, in order to emphasize even more the good results that our algorithm obtained.

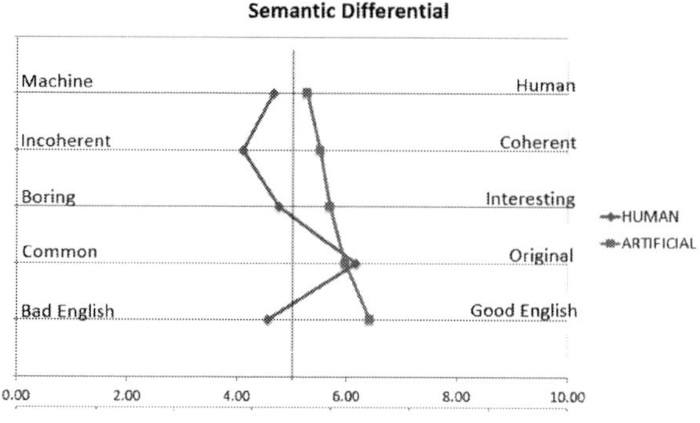

Figure 7: Total semantic differential based on the total population responses.

7 Conclusions

Our evaluation suggests that we achieved the general objective proposed by avoiding an over-structured text and generating coherent stories with novel sentences based on what was previously written and also by creating a narrative flow in texts resulting in coherent stories.

The proposed architecture is an entire methodology that converts a single word into a whole story, by using syntactic and semantic characteristics of words and phrases, thus building a bridge between language syntax and semantics.

We proposed an architecture for generating texts that resemble in a better way the language that is used in fiction texts, and we called this *literary style*. Likewise, we managed to imitate creativity in the sense that we do not have control of the contents of the stories, and it is not possible to know the outcome of the algorithm until it creates a new narrative arc, all of this based on a single word as an input.

Nevertheless, we need to be cautious about our results. We specifically rely on the assumption that most of the meaning that a text holds is created in the mind of the reader. By doing this, we avoid the problem of producing texts with intentionality, and focused on language experiments and guided word combinatory. We successfully avoided the production of text that gives an artificial feeling to the reader, and manages to hold style while being creative at the same time.

References

Steven Bird, Edward Loper, and Ewan Klein. 2009. *Natural Language Processing with Python*. O'Reilly Media Inc.

Umberto Eco. 2005. Sobre algunas funciones de la literatura. In Helena Lozano Miralles, editor, *Sobre Literatura*, chapter 1, pages 9–23. Debolsillo.

Maria Teresa Espinal, Josep Macia, Jaime Mateu, and Josep Quer. 2014. *Semantica*. Akal.

Christiane Fellbaum. 1998. *WordNet: An Electronic Lexical Database*. Bradford Books.

Pablo Gervás. 2013. Propp's morphology of the folk tale as a grammar for generation. *Computational Models of Narrative*.

Jay J. Jiang and David W. Conrath. 1997. Semantic similarity based on corpus statistics and lexical taxonomy. *Proceedings of International Conference Research on Computational Linguistics, 15*.

Andrej Karpathy. 2015. The unreasonable effectiveness of recurrent neural networks. http://karpathy.github.io/2015/05/21/rnn-effectiveness/.

Dan Klein and Christopher D. Manning. 2003. Accurate unlexicalized parsing. In *Proceedings of the 41st Meeting of the Association for Computational Linguistics*, pages 423–430.

Neil McIntyre and Mirella Lapata. 2009. Learning to tell tales: A data-driven approach to story generation. *Proceedings of the 47th Annual Meeting of the Association for Computational Linguistics*.

James R. Meehan. 1977. Tale-spin an interactive program that writes stories. *Proceedings of the 5th International Conference on Artificial Intelligence*.

Charles E. Osgood, George Suci, and Percy Tannenbaum. 1957. *The measurement of meaning*. University of Illinois Press.

Thomas E. Payne. 2011. *Understanding English Grammar: a linguistic introduction*. Cambridge University Press.

Rafael Pérez. 1999. Mexica: A computer model of creativity in writing.

Steven Pinker. 2014. *The sense of style: the thinking person's guide to writing in the 21st century*. Penguin Group.

Edhud Reiter and Robert Dale. 2000. *Building Natural Language Generation Systems*. Cambridge University Press.

Ivo Swartjes and Mariet Theune. 2006. A fabula model for emergent narrative. In *Technologies for Interactive Digital Storytelling and Entertainment Conference*, pages 49–60. Springer.

Perry Thorndyke. 1977. Cognitive structures in comprehension and memory of narrative discourse. *Cognitive Psychology*, pages 77–110.

Intersecting Word Vectors to Take Figurative Language to New Heights

Andrea Gagliano & Emily Paul & Kyle Booten & Marti A. Hearst
University of California at Berkeley
{andrea.gagliano,emily.paul,kbooten,hearst}@berkeley.edu

Abstract

This paper proposes a technique to create figurative relationships using Mikolov et al.'s word vectors. Drawing on existing work on figurative language, we start with a pair of words and use the intersection of word vector similarity sets to blend the distinct semantic spaces of the two words. We conduct preliminary quantitative and qualitative observations to compare the use of this novel intersection method with the standard word vector addition method for the purpose of supporting the generation of figurative language.

1 Introduction

> *"I sit in my chair all day and work and work*
> *Measuring words against each other."*
> - Conrad Aiken *Improvisations: Light And Snow*

While metaphors are part of everyday language, in poetry they are vital. Metaphorical language, in contrast with literal or non-metaphorical language, "mak[es] use of structure imported from a completely different conceptual domain" (Lakoff and Turner, 1989).

Lakoff and Turner analyze famous poems and show how they can be understood as the blending of concepts from multiple metaphorical frames. For example, they state that a common metaphor is DEATH AS DEPARTURE and provide an example of an Emily Dickinson poem in which she merely needs to mention the words "death" and "carriage" in the same set of stanzas for the reader to know that the carriage is not taking a spin around the block, but rather a one-way trip with no return.

> *"Because I could not stop for Death –*
> *He kindly stopped for me –*

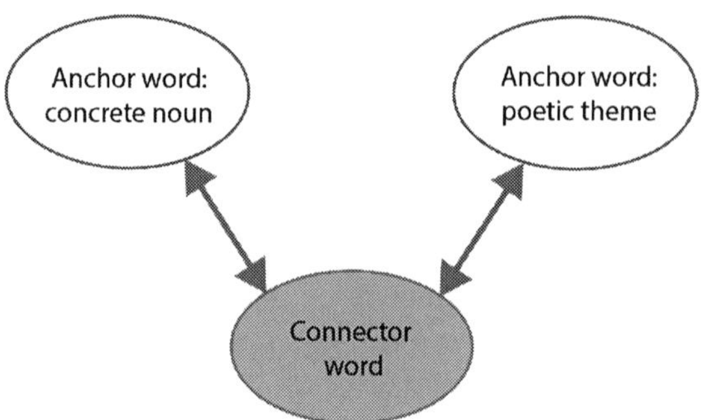

Figure 1: Connector word drawing together the two semantic spaces of the anchor words.

> *The Carriage held but just Ourselves –*
> *And Immortality."*

Lakoff and Turner convincingly argue that there are basic conceptual metaphors that hold for how we conceive of, and therefore talk about, death (e.g., DEATH IS WINTER, DEATH IS REST or DEATH IS FREEDOM FROM BONDAGE) and these are combined in poetry with other metaphors, such as LIFE IS A JOURNEY, A LIFETIME IS A YEAR, NIGHT IS A COVER, PEOPLE ARE PLANTS, and so on. Our goal in this work is to develop new methods of automatically suggesting words that link together concepts across semantic spaces or frames, and so to aid both programs and people in the generation of poetic and figurative language.

We add to the body of work on poetry analysis and generation by exploring a method to generate a set of words (connector words) that can be used to create a figurative relationship with a pair of anchor words, as shown in Figure 1. We do this by making use of recent advances in statistical word similarity generation methods, in particular the word2vec embedding technology.

Mikolov et al.'s work on word representations in

Proceedings of the Fifth Workshop on Computational Linguistics for Literature, NAACL-HLT 2016, pages 20–31,
San Diego, California, June 1, 2016. ©2016 Association for Computational Linguistics

Anchor word pairs	Connector words
surrendering & storm	barrage
caring & flame	cook
life & road	journey

Table 1: Examples of anchor word pairs and connector words. *Life & road* connected by *journey* is an example of how the framework in Figure 1 maps to Lakoff's LIFE IS A JOURNEY metaphor.

vector space, actualized in the word2vec technology, identifies semantic relationships between words using word vector algebra. These word vectors perform remarkably well at identifying semantic analogy relationships, e.g., capital city to country, currency to country, city to state, and man to woman (Mikolov et al., 2013a; Mikolov et al., 2013b; Mikolov et al., 2013c). The classic example showcasing the power of the word vector algebra is:

vector('King') - vector('Man') + vector('Woman')
= vector that is closest to *vector('Queen')*

In this paper, we extend the use of these vectors beyond their primary application of identifying such analogous type relationships: we explore their use to draw together two semantic spaces for the creation of *figurative* relationships.

Specifically, starting with a pair of anchor words, made up of a concrete noun and a poetic theme, we leverage Mikolov et al.'s word vectors to return the sets of words most similar to either anchor word in the pair. By finding the intersection of these two sets, we can identify connector words that draw together the anchor words to create figurative relationships. Some examples of the anchor and connector words can be seen in Table 1.

For each pair of anchor words we also generate a list of suggested connector words by using Mikolov et al.'s word vector algebra. We then quantitatively observe the difference between the lists of connector words produced by intersection and by addition. For the connector words from the intersection list, we observe a more balanced similarity score between the connector words and each anchor word than we do for the connector words from the addition list. We then construct an initial dataset to explore qualitatively the figurative relationships generated using connector words from the addition list and those

generated using connector words from the intersection list.

The remainder of this paper provides an overview of related work on figurative language and semantic relationships; outlines the computational methods used to retrieve connector words; describes quantitative and qualitative observations of the retrieved connector words; and discusses future work.

2 Related work

2.1 Work on figurative language

"Figurative language," in particular metaphor, plays a crucial role in poetry. Lakoff and Turner (1989) explicate in great detail how metaphors are combined in everyday language, and how poets extend and elaborate on conventional metaphors in new ways. A metaphor can be thought of as a linguistic structure that creates a "mapping" of two conceptual spaces or frames (Lakoff and Turner, 1989) or the "blending" of two input spaces (Fauconnier and Turner, 2008). Veale et al. (2000) point to this as an important theoretical model for computational work on metaphor, and emphasize the highly structured relationships that metaphors create between two terms. In one of their examples, to see *Scientists* as *Priests* metaphorically could mean to see their *lab-benches* as *altars*. In this case, the general terms are metaphorically connected based on some more specific attribute that is common to each. This commonality, however, is not immediately obvious, so a good metaphor reveals something surprising about a conceptual space by combining it with another conceptual space.

Veale et al. (2000) offer examples of systems that create such relationships between two input terms to form metaphors. More recently, researchers have generated poetic metaphorical relationships between two terms by leveraging large corpora. Veale and Hao (2007) found metaphorical relationships between two terms by mining Google search results for adjectives used to describe both terms. Veale and Hao (2008) applied a similar approach to mine more complex metaphors from WordNet. Such techniques have been deployed in "computer poetry" applications that automatically generate verse (Veale, 2013; Harmon, 2015).

Literary theorist William Empson (2004) argued

for the importance of reading the "ambiguities" present in verse. The most basic type of ambiguity occurs when a metaphor simultaneously draws on different qualities of the items brought into metaphorical relation, and so it is "effective in several ways at once." For instance, *eyes* are like *sun* for multiple reasons (e.g., both are literally round, and both may be "bright"). More complicated ambiguities may be generated through puns, in which a word simultaneously carries two distinct and ironically opposite meanings, each relevant to the context. To use Empson's example: in Pope's *Dunciad*, a character sleeping "in port" may be both safe at harbor and drunk (on port wine). In this case, two distinct conceptual spaces are activated by one word.

Furthermore, as Empson argues, poets themselves are not always fully in control of the meanings of their words and, "discovering his idea in the act of writing" may create "a simile which applies to nothing exactly, but lies half-way between two things," a subtly mixed metaphor. He gives the example of a passage from a verse-play by John Ford in which the term "gall" at first seems to mean "boldness"—but, when the author later mentions a "well-grown oak," comes to retroactively signal "oak-galls," a horticultural disease. "Figurative language" is not merely the sort of ordered and symmetrical matching of cognitive structures evinced by clear metaphors; it is also what happens when poets get caught up in loose and chaotic association between words, the way jazz musicians zig and zag between notes.

2.2 Semantic relationships from word embeddings

Distributional approaches to representing word meaning have a long history in computational linguistics, and are motivated by the notion that "You shall know a word by the company it keeps!" (Firth, 1957) and the Wittgenstein-inspired notion that a concept is not an isolated thing but really a constellation of concepts linked by family resemblances (Rosch and Mervis, 1975).

Schütze (1993) made early attempts to represent the meaning of concepts by creating n-dimensional word spaces. More recent attempts which use larger collections and innovations in algorithms have yielded more accurate representations of semantic relatedness. These include Mikolov et al.'s work on word embeddings learned using a Continuous Skip-gram Model. It extends beyond bag-of-words models by accounting for the context a word appears in. This model is implemented in Google's word2vec tool[1] which has shown significant success in finding both syntactic and semantic relationships between words (Mikolov et al., 2013b; Mikolov et al., 2013a; Mikolov et al., 2013c).

Mikolov et al. find semantic relationships from word pairs which can be categorized into 79 specific word relations, such as *Cause:Effect* or *Action:Goal* as identified in the SemEval-2012 Task 2, *Measuring Relation Similarity* (Jurgens et al., 2012; Turney, 2012). For example, the word pair *clothing:shirt* falls into the *Class Inclusion:Singular Collective* relation. Mikolov et al. (2013c) then use a vector offset technique to understand the validity of resulting analogous relationships, such as "*clothing* is to *shirt* as *dish* is to *bowl*" as tested against the word relation data set presented by Jurgens et al. (2012). Similarly, our work aims to identify a semantic relationship between two words. It differs in that we aim to find figurative relationships between two words for poetic purposes, as opposed to analogous relationships between two pairs of words.

3 Computational methods in word2vec to retrieve connector words

In this section we outline two methods – an addition model and an intersection model – to retrieve connector words that support figurative relationships using word2vec.

The standard functionality of word2vec is to retrieve the top-ranked most similar words. Word2vec addition is optimized for such tasks, but here we are more interested in retrieving words to support figurative relationships. We aim to find the words in the overlap of the family resemblance spaces of each of the anchor words.

We do so by retrieving words from word2vec similarity lists that are common to each anchor word. In contrast to the addition model, the intersection model retrieves words from further down on the sim-

---

[1]Throughout this paper, we are using the Gensim implementation of word2vec (Řehůřek and Sojka, 2010), trained on 'pruned.word2vec.txt'.

Concrete nouns		
bed	ear	finger
horse	sand	hair
bell	grass	rock
book	rose	breast
ship	blood	window
wing	girl	snow
wood	ring	body
room	wine	ground
mouth	garden	stone
storm	brain	flame
town	wave	shadow
silver	mist	line
stream	dawn	path
dust	breath	king
color	spring	darkness
side	nation	race
state		

Table 2: Pool of concrete nouns used in the selection of anchor pairs.

Poetic themes		
loss	melancholy	anger
animals	calmness	compassion
confusion	death	envy
faith	fear	forgiveness
freedom	friendship	god
grace	gratitude	grief
hate	hope	immortality
jealousy	joy	life
mothers	nature	peace
people	religion	remembrance
love	sadness	silence
smiling	songs	spirituality
spring	suffering	truth
unity	vanity	war
water	wind	bitterness
consciousness	happiness	earth
soul	surrender	violence

Table 3: Pool of poetic themes used in the selection of anchor pairs.

ilarity lists for each anchor word (moving towards the outer edges of their respective family resemblance spaces). The resulting words in the shared space maintain a balance between the two anchor words, thus drawing them together.

To narrow the scope, the work in this paper focuses on anchor word pairs comprising one concrete noun and one poetic theme. We chose this focus from our observations that poetry often relies on a connection between a concrete concept and a more abstract theme, which is consistent with Kao and Jurafsky's (2015) findings that professional poetry contains more concreteness.

3.1 Selecting anchor word pairs

For the investigation here, we randomly generate anchor word pairs from a list of concrete nouns (see Table 2) and a list of poetic themes[2] (see Table 3).[3]

The set of concrete nouns comes from existing poetry.[4] The words are selected based on their word frequency across the corpus, number of noun senses in WordNet (WordNet, 2010), and degree of concreteness using the word concreteness dataset developed by Brysbaert et al. (2013). The frequency measure is normalized across the corpus. The mean concreteness ratings from Brysbaert et al. (2013) range from 0.0 to 5.0 and include standard deviations. The concrete noun list is composed of nouns with a normalized frequency ranging from 0.0 to 0.1; the number of noun senses ranging from 0 to 4; and the degree of concreteness ranging from 3.5 to 5.0, with the degree of concreteness standard deviation ranging from 0.0 to 3.0.

In generating anchor word pairs, we randomly select a concrete noun and a poetic theme pair where the two words occupy distinct semantic spaces. For the purposes of this paper, we use a cosine similarity score of less than 0.4 as a threshold. The similarity scores of candidate concrete nouns to candidate poetic themes range from -0.15 (dissimilar) to 0.45

---

[2]Created from a list of poetic themes from http://www.poetseers.org/themes/ then expanded to include the top 5 most similar words, using word2vec. The expanded list was normalized to lower-case words. Overly-specific words, including "rainbows", "cats," "pets," "rabbits," "dogs," "Iraq," and "sewage", were removed.

[3]These particular lists were chosen for expediency; the rigorous definition of concrete nouns and poetic themes is not central to our exploration.

[4]Existing poetry from a corpus of 2,860 poems downloaded from the "19th Century American Poetry" section of http://famouspoetsandpoems.com.

Top 10 words from word2vec addition for storm + surrendering
surrendered
hurricane
storms
snowstorm
rainstorm
tornado
blizzard
typhoon
twister
squall

Table 4: Top 10 words retrieved when adding anchor words *storm* and *surrendering* using word2vec addition.

(similar). This similarity check is used to create an anchor word pair comprising two words with different semantic spaces. If the two anchor words are too similar, they will rely on a synonymous connection and thus will not provide two distinct semantic spaces to blend.

3.2 Addition model in word2vec to retrieve connector words

The addition model retrieves a set of connector words which are the most similar to a pair of anchor words using word2vec's existing vector addition approach.

Implementation of this addition model involves starting with word2vec's word vector representations of the concrete noun, $\vec{c}$, and the poetic theme, $\vec{t}$, of the anchor word pair.

The word vector, $\vec{a}$, is then defined such that $\vec{a} = \vec{c} + \vec{t}$. Word2vec then searches for the word vectors with the greatest cosine similarity to $\vec{a}$, which approximates their similarity (Mikolov et al., 2013c). We use this vector addition to find a set A containing n words closest to $\vec{a}$. For example, if we take the concrete noun "storm" and the poetic theme "surrendering" as an anchor word pair, we can retrieve the list of words in Table 4.[5]

The resulting list contains primarily words that are synonyms to one of the two anchor words. However, our goal is to retrieve connector words

that blend the semantic spaces of the two anchor words, so we investigate an alternative computation in word2vec, the intersection model.

3.3 Intersection model in word2vec to retrieve connector words

For the intersection model, we start with word2vec's vector representations of the concrete noun, $\vec{c}$, and the poetic theme, $\vec{t}$, of the anchor word pair.

Using word2vec, we then find a set, C, which contains the top $n = 1000$ word vectors that have the greatest cosine similarity to $\vec{c}$. Similarly, we find a set, T, which contains the top $n = 1000$ word vectors that have the greatest cosine similarity to $\vec{t}$.

Looking at the intersection, I, of the two sets $I = C \cap T$, we find words that relate both to the initial concrete noun, $(\vec{c})$, and the poetic theme, $(\vec{t})$.

The resulting set, I, varies significantly in size depending on the concrete noun and poetic theme pair chosen. The depth n also contributes to the size of the set, I. In our analyses, we elected to use $n = 1000$ because it elicited plentiful yet meaningful results.

It is the case that for any sets I and A of similar size, there are likely to be words unique to each set, as well as words that are shared between these sets. A proof of this appears in Appendix A.

Since A and I have overlapping words, but also contain unique words, we remove the overlapping words to focus on the resulting set $U_I = I \setminus A$, containing the words unique to the intersection set, and $U_A = A \setminus I$, containing the words unique to the addition set. We focus on these unique words sets to facilitate our observations of the differences between the two models. Quantitatively, we observe differences in the range of similarity scores between the anchor word-connector word pairs. Qualitatively, we use the unique words from each set to consider the potential to support figurative language by combining the semantic spaces of the two anchor words.

With the example anchor words, *storm* and *surrendering*, we see the resulting unique word lists in Table 5. In the next two sections we quantitatively and qualitatively observe these two lists.

---

[5]Proper nouns were removed from the list and morphological duplicates removed.

Unique to Intersection $U_I = I \setminus A$	Unique to Addition $U_A = A \setminus I$
onslaught	squall
stranding	tornado
blowing	typhoon
dissipating	snowstorm
battering	flooding
game	rainstorm
breastworks	deluge
regrouped	downpour
batter	blizzard
dissipated	ike
outburst	twister
pounding	hurricane
submerging	rain
pounded	
barrage	
regrouping	
stalemate	

Table 5: Connector words for *storm* and *surrendering* retrieved from the words unique to I and the words unique to A.

Unique to Addition $U_I = I \setminus A$	Similarity to noun *storm*	Similarity to theme *surrendering*
onslaught	0.30	0.20
stranding	0.27	0.28
blowing	0.24	0.29
dissipating	0.23	0.22
battering	0.29	0.24
game	0.19	0.25
breastworks	0.19	0.20
regrouped	0.19	0.31
batter	0.22	0.25
dissipated	0.24	0.21
outburst	0.21	0.20
pounding	0.20	0.26
submerging	0.26	0.23
pounded	0.24	0.32
barrage	0.25	0.20
regrouping	0.19	0.31
stalemate	0.19	0.21
Average spread between similarity scores: 0.05		

Table 6: Similarity scores between connector words found in U_I to anchor words *storm* and *surrendering*. The average spread between the scores of 0.05 indicates the small band of similarity the words exist in, showing the balanced similarity the connector word has with each of the anchor words.

4 Quantitative observations of retrieved connector words

In observing the cosine similarities between the words in U_I and each anchor word, and the words in U_A and each anchor word, we begin to see a pattern where the words from U_I fall within a smaller band of similarity than of those in U_A (see Tables 6 and 7 for example with words from Table 5). Note that the highest possible cosine similarity score is 1, indicating maximum similarity, and the lowest is -1, indicating dissimilarity.

Across 10 different randomly selected anchor word pairs, we see that this same pattern holds. The words in U_I fall within a band of similarity ranging from approximately 0.25 to approximately 0.30 where the average spread between the two similarities is 0.06. By comparison, the similarities between connector words in U_A and each anchor word falls within a larger band of similarity ranging from approximately 0.1 to approximately 0.6 where the average spread between the two similarities is 0.44. Table 8 shows these ranges for each anchor word pair. The connector words in U_I are more balanced between both of the anchor words, whereas the connector words in U_A are more closely related to a single anchor word.

5 Qualitative observations of retrieved connector words

Next we qualitatively explore the potential of each model to retrieve words in the shared space between two anchor words using a crowd-sourced dataset of figurative relationships. We annotate these relationships based on the types of connections made between the connector words and anchor word pairs.

5.1 Dataset construction

We construct a dataset made up of sentences stating the figurative relationships tying the connector words from the addition and intersection lists to pairs of anchor words. This dataset allows us to explore the potential of the connector words pro-

Unique to Intersection $U_A = I \setminus A$	Similarity to noun *storm*	Similarity to theme *surrendering*
squall	0.63	-0.03
tornado	0.64	-0.02
typhoon	0.62	-0.01
snowstorm	0.64	0.01
flooding	0.57	0.01
rainstorm	0.57	0.07
deluge	0.50	0.08
downpour	0.52	0.08
blizzard	0.61	0.00
ike	0.58	0.02
twister	0.62	-0.01
hurricane	0.73	0.04
rain	0.46	0.10
Average spread between similarity scores: 0.56		

Table 7: Similarity scores between connector words found in U_A to anchor words *storm* and *surrendering*. The average spread between the scores of 0.56 shows the wide range of similarity scores.

Anchor word pairs	Range of avg. sim. from words in U_I to anchor words	Range of avg. sim. from words in U_A to anchor words
flame & caring	$0.22 - 0.30$	$0.13 - 0.58$
color & earthly	$0.28 - 0.32$	$0.17 - 0.55$
hair & anguish	$0.27 - 0.33$	$0.14 - 0.66$
flame & killing	$0.23 - 0.26$	$0.09 - 0.55$
mouth & comp.	$0.25 - 0.29$	$0.16 - 0.54$
storm & surr.	$0.21 - 0.26$	$0.03 - 0.69$
ring & mankind	$0.21 - 0.34$	$0.11 - 0.57$
hair & envied	$0.27 - 0.31$	$0.17 - 0.58$
book & liberties	$0.23 - 0.29$	$0.15 - 0.54$
town & grieving	$0.24 - 0.28$	$0.14 - 0.54$

Table 8: The low end of the ranges is the average of the minimum similarity scores across all the connector words to each of the words in the anchor word pair. The upper end of the ranges is the average of the maximums. A smaller range means that the anchor words have more balanced similarity to the connector word. comp. = compassionate; surr. = surrendering.

vided by each approach to blend the distinct semantic spaces of the two anchor words. To generate this dataset, we presented crowd-sourced workers from Mechanical Turk with a list of words, either those unique to the I set (U_I) or those unique to the A set (U_A). The words in the provided sets were normalized to exclude proper nouns, lower-case all characters, and eliminate morphological duplicates. If the unique word list exceeded 10 words, a random sample of 10 words was shown.

The Mechanical Turk workers then selected a single connector word from the list and wrote a sentence to describe the relationship between the anchor words and the connector word. Mechanical Turk workers were provided the diagram in Figure 1 with the concrete noun and poetic theme words populated. We informed workers that they should select the connector word that "best connects the anchor words in a poetic sense (e.g., using a double meaning, creating a new image, creating an interesting relationship, etc.)".

The workers were prompted to fill in text to complete a template sentence of the form: "[connector word] connects [concrete noun] and [poetic theme]

because...". For example, "Barrage connects storm and surrendering because...".

With 25 workers writing 4 sentences each across 10 anchor word pairs, the constructed dataset contained 100 generated sentences.

The following sections provide examples of the figurative relationships among the selected connector word and anchor word pairs created by Mechanical Turk workers and discussion of whether the relationships created achieve heightened effects by drawing together two distinct semantic spaces.

5.2 Sample data

Using the dataset of generated sentences, we explore the potential for word2vec to provide connector words that blend the two distinct semantic spaces of the two anchor words using the addition and intersection operations.

Below, we present detailed results for 3 of the assessed anchor word pairs. We show which words were chosen by Mechanical Turk workers as the best connector word (bolded), and the sentences describing the relationship among the connector word

Unique to Intersection	Unique to Addition
radiant	celestial
reflections	**hues**
clearness	uncolored
unclouded	metaphysical
blackness	astral
loveliness	cosmic
refracted	translucence
eidetic	divine
allusiveness	heavenly
creeds	
geometrical	
exquisiteness	
diaphanous	

Table 9: Figurative ties between *color* and *earthly*. Bolded words were selected by Mechanical Turk workers as the best word to create the figurative tie.

and the anchor words (underlined) as created by the workers.

5.2.1 Sample 1: color and earthly

All connector words chosen are shown in Table 9. Sample connection descriptions from Mechanical Turk workers as follows:

"**Radiant** connects color and earthly because radiant means a bright color that looks like it's shining and at night, the earthly sky is radiant because it shines brightly with the stars."

"**Hues** connects color and earthly because hues imply various colors, shades, or characteristics and hues can be earthly in tone, such as blues, greens and browns."

5.2.2 Sample 2: storm and surrendering

All connector words chosen are shown in Table 10. Sample connection descriptions from Mechanical Turk workers are as follows:

"**Barrage** connects storm and surrendering because a storm is a barrage of bad weather like winds and rain people surrender when they feel a barrage of overwhelming things coming at them."

"**Hurricane** connects storm and surrendering because it is a type of storm and those who surrender to it are spared, like grass and those who stand against it are devastated, like big trees."

Unique to Intersection	Unique to Addition
onslaught	squall
stranding	tornado
blowing	**typhoon**
dissipating	snowstorm
battering	flooding
game	rainstorm
breastworks	deluge
regrouped	downpour
batter	blizzard
dissipated	ike
outburst	twister
pounding	**hurricane**
submerging	rain
pounded	
barrage	
regrouping	
stalemate	

Table 10: Figurative ties between *storm* and *surrendering*. Bolded words were selected by Mechanical Turk workers as the best word to create the figurative tie.

5.2.3 Sample 3: flame and caring

All connector words chosen are shown in Table 11. Sample connection descriptions from Mechanical Turk workers are as follows:

"**Cook** connects caring and flame because it is related to flame as flames are used in cooking and cooking can be a symbol of caring for someone with good food."

"**Torch** connects caring and flame because when someone cares about someone else it's often said they are carrying a torch for them, while the visual of a torch itself tends to have a flame atop it."

5.3 Discussion of qualitative observations

As stated above, our goal in suggesting connector words is to blend the distinct semantic spaces of the two anchor words to create figurative relationships.

While the sentences with synonyms do contain figurative language, they do not achieve our goal of using the connector word to blend the two anchor words. Instead, the connector word shares a

Unique to Intersection	Unique to Addition
affection	compassion
friendship	**torch**
spirit	selfless
passion	considerate
soul	kindness
brotherhood	compassionate
aloneness	loving
love	**devotion**
cook	
undying	

Table 11: Figurative ties between *flame* and *caring*. Bolded words were selected by Mechanical Turk workers as the best word to create the figurative tie.

semantic space with one of the anchor words and this shared semantic space is then blended with the semantic space of the other anchor word. The sentences reflect a figurative relationship that is present between the two anchor words (which does not depend on the connector word) rather than a new space created by the introduction of the connector word.

We observe that the connector words that create a heightened effect by blending the two anchor words have a balanced cosine similarity to both anchor words (in the range of approximately 0.25 to approximately 0.30 as discussed in section 4 and shown in Table 8). This means that the connector word is not closer to one or the other anchor word, but rather occupies the shared space between the two anchor words. In contrast, the connector words that are synonymous with one of the anchor words, and thus do not blend the semantic spaces of the two anchor words, have imbalanced cosine similarities to the two anchor words. The connector word's shared semantic space with one of the anchor words is visible in a higher cosine similarity to that anchor word (approximately 0.6) and a much lower cosine similarity to the other anchor word (approximately 0.1). In this latter case, the connector word is not blending the semantic spaces of the two anchor words but is rather sharing the semantic space of one.

5.3.1 Relationships based on synonyms

In the sentences that rely on synonyms for one part of the relationship, the connector word has a metaphorical relationship with one of the anchor words and a non-metaphorical with the other anchor word.

By looking at word2vec similarity scores of concrete noun to connector word and poetic theme to connector word, we can see that in the relationships that rely on synonym there is a relatively wide spread between the similarity scores.

The examples below show figurative relationships that rely on synonym-based relationships between the connector word and one of the anchor words along with the similarity scores between the connector word and the concrete noun and between the connector word and the poetic theme.

Examples:

"**Torch** connects caring and flame because caring for someone can feel like a flame or a torch burns inside you for them."

Torch and flame are connected through a synonymous relationship; these two words are then connected to caring through a metaphor (caring is a torch burning)

Similarity score **torch**-caring: 0.06

Similarity score **torch**-flame: 0.67

"**Hues** connects color and earthly because hues imply various colors, shades, or characteristics and hues can be earthly in tone, such as blues, greens and browns."

Hues and color are connected through a synonymous relationship; these two words are then connected to earthly through a metaphor (colors are earthly).

Similarity score **hues**-color: 0.61

Similarity score **hues**-earthly: 0.09

5.3.2 Relationships blending distinct semantic spaces

The figurative relationships that result in a heightened effect are created through a connector word retrieved from the overlapping semantic space between the two anchor words.

In these relationships, the word2vec similarity scores of concrete noun to connector word and poetic theme to connector word are close, indicating a balanced relationship.

The examples below show figurative relationships that use a connector word that blends the two distinct semantic spaces of the anchor words.

Examples:

"**Barrage** connects storm and surrendering because a storm is a barrage of bad weather like winds and rain people surrender when they feel a barrage of overwhelming things coming at them."

A storm is a barrage of bad weather and life can be a barrage to which you surrender.

Similarity score **barrage**-storm: 0.25

Similarity score **barrage**-surrendering: 0.20

"**Cook** connects caring and flame because it is related to flame as flames are used in cooking and cooking can be a symbol of caring for someone with good food."

Providing nourishment by cooking requires flames and is caring.

Similarity score **cook**-caring: 0.26

Similarity score **cook**-flame: 0.22

6 Summary of observations

In the dataset of sentences generated by Mechanical Turk workers drawing the connections between anchor words and connector words, we observe the following:

- Instances where the cosine similarity scores between each of the anchor words and the connector word are unbalanced tend to lead to a synonymous relationship between one anchor word-connector word pair (a nonmetaphorical relation) and a shared figurative relationship with the second anchor word (a metaphorical relation). In these cases the connector word is not drawing together the family resemblance semantic spaces of the two anchor words, because it already exists in the semantic space of one of them.

- Instances where the cosine similarity scores between each of the anchor words and the connector word are balanced tend to lead to a heightened effect relationship blending the two distinct semantic spaces of the anchor word.

As seen in Table 8, the band of similarity scores resulting from words in U_I is smaller than the band of similarity resulting from connector words in U_A, suggesting a more balanced relationship.

7 Future work

We have observed figurative relationships resulting from the introduction of a connector word to an anchor word pair. We notice that balanced cosine similarity scores between the connector word and each anchor word tend to lead to heightened effects by blending the two distinct semantic spaces of the anchor word.

The words unique to the intersection list proposed here have balanced cosine similarity scores ranging from approximately 0.25 to 0.30, suggesting that finding the words unique to the intersection list prioritizes the retrieval of words that blend the distinct semantic spaces of two anchor words.

The next step in this work is to test this hypothesis with an evaluation. Such an evaluation may include looking at the band of similarity from 0.25 to 0.30 directly, by way of the unique words to intersection and unique words to addition sets, and/or by way of the complete intersection and complete addition sets. We could also conduct threshold testing for varying word2vec settings and top n settings. In evaluating this work, it would be interesting to see if everyday people and practicing poets judge the relationships differently.

Additionally, through further evaluation, the nature of other bands of similarity outside of the 0.25 to 0.30 range could be tested, as well as the presence of such a band of similarity when expanding beyond the concrete noun-poetic theme scope.

Expanding beyond the concrete noun-poetic theme scope could also involve grounding the anchor pair selection more explicitly in the metaphors proposed by Lakoff and Turner (1989).

Further related work may include consideration of more computations within word2vec to see what types of word relations such computations support.

Once a conceptual understanding is more established, research could then be conducted regarding the various applications that such findings could be used for. Such applications may include poetry generation or tools to assist in creative writing.

Overall, we hope that this work will continue to promote the development of computational approaches to figurative language, because:

> "By metaphor you paint
> A thing."
>
> - Wallace Stevens *Poem Written At Morning*

Acknowledgements

We thank David Bamman for his guidance and valuable insight,s and the reviewers for their very thoughtful and thorough feedback.

A   Appendix: Proof

Formally, the set A contains the top n most similar word vectors, $\vec{w}$, such that $cos(\vec{w}, \vec{a}) \geq \alpha$, where α is a minimum similarity threshold resulting from selecting the top n words. As such:

$$\vec{w} \in A, s.t. :$$

$$cos(\vec{w}, \vec{a}) = cos(\vec{w}, (\vec{c} + \vec{t})) = \frac{\vec{w} \cdot (\vec{c} + \vec{t})}{|\vec{w}|\,|\vec{c} + \vec{t}|} \geq \alpha \tag{1}$$

The set I contains all word vectors, $\vec{w}$, such that $cos(\vec{w}, \vec{c}) \geq \beta$ and $cos(\vec{w}, \vec{t}) \geq \gamma$, where β and γ are minimum similarity thresholds resulting from selecting the top n words from each list.

$$\vec{w} \in I, s.t. :$$

$$cos(\vec{w}, \vec{c}) = \frac{\vec{w} \cdot \vec{c}}{|\vec{w}|\,|\vec{c}|} \geq \beta$$
$$cos(\vec{w}, \vec{t}) = \frac{\vec{w} \cdot \vec{t}}{|\vec{w}|\,|\vec{t}|} \geq \gamma \tag{2}$$

If we were finding the single word vector that maximized (1) and (2), the two equations would be equivalent, as shown by Levy and Goldberg (2014). Rather, in the addition model, we are finding the set of words that satisfy (1), and, in the intersection model, we are finding the set of words that satisfy (2). We can see that (1) and (2) are not necessarily equivalent. If they were, we would have a connector word, $\vec{w}$, such that (1) and (2) were always both satisfied. As such, we would need to satisfy (3):

$$cos(\vec{w}, (\vec{c} + \vec{t})) \geq \alpha$$
$$cos(\vec{w}, \vec{c}) \geq \beta \tag{3}$$
$$cos(\vec{w}, \vec{t}) \geq \gamma$$

Note that (3) assumes the word vectors are length-normalized. We then expand (3) as follows:

$$w_1 * (c_1 + t_1) + w_2 * (c_2 + t_2)$$
$$+ ... + w_n * (c_n + t_n) \geq \alpha$$
$$w_1 * c_1 + w_2 * c_2 +$$
$$+ ... + w_n * c_n \geq \beta \tag{4}$$
$$w_1 * t_1 + w_2 * t_2$$
$$+ ... + w_n * t_n \geq \gamma$$

We can solve (4) as follows:

$$\beta + \gamma \geq \alpha \tag{5}$$

(5) is not necessarily always true. Thus, the initial assumption that the addition and intersection models contain the same word vectors is contradicted, which confirms that A does not necessarily equal I.

References

[Brysbaert et al.2013] Marc Brysbaert, Amy Beth Warriner, and Victor Kuperman. 2013. Concreteness Ratings for 40 Thousand Generally Known English Words and Lemmas. In *Behavior Research Methods*, pages 1–8.

[Empson2004] William Empson. 2004. *Seven types of ambiguity*, volume 645. Random House.

[Fauconnier and Turner2008] Gilles Fauconnier and Mark Turner. 2008. *The way we think: Conceptual blending and the mind's hidden complexities*. Basic Books.

[Firth1957] John Rupert Firth. 1957. A synopsis of linguistic theory, 1930-1955. *Studies in linguistic analysis (Special volume of the Philological Society)*, pages 1–31. Reprinted in: Frank R. Palmer (ed.) *Selected papers of J. R. Firth 1952-59*, Longmans, Green and Co Ltd, London and Harlow, UK, 168-205; citation on page 179.

[Harmon2015] Sarah Harmon. 2015. Figure8: A novel system for generating and evaluating figurative language. In *Proceedings of the Sixth International Conference on Computational Creativity June*, page 71.

[Jurgens et al.2012] David Jurgens, Saif Mohammad, Peter Turney, and Keith Holyoak. 2012. Semeval-2012 task 2: Measuring degrees of relational similarity. In *In *SEM 2012: The First Joint Conference on Lexical and Computational Semantics (SemEval 2012)*, page 356364. Association for Computational Linguistics.

[Kao and Jurafsky2015] Justine Kao and Dan Jurafsky. 2015. A computational analysis of poetic style: Imagism and its influence on modern professional and amateur poetry. *Linguistic Issues in Language Technology*, 12(3).

[Lakoff and Turner1989] George Lakoff and Mark Turner. 1989. *More than cool reason: A field guide to poetic metaphor*. University of Chicago Press.

[Levy and Goldberg2014] Omer Levy and Yoav Goldberg. 2014. Linguistic Regularities in Sparse and Explicit Word Representations. In *CoNLL*.

[Mikolov et al.2013a] Tomas Mikolov, Kai Chen, Greg Corrado, Jeffrey Dean, and Dan Jurafsky. 2013a. Efficient Estimation of Word Representations in Vector Space. In *arXiv preprint arXiv:1301.3781*.

[Mikolov et al.2013b] Tomas Mikolov, Ilya Sutskever, Kai Chen, Greg Corrado, and Jeffrey Dean. 2013b. Distributed Representations of Words and Phrases and their Compositionality. In *arXiv:1310.4546 [cs.CL]*.

[Mikolov et al.2013c] Tomas Mikolov, Wen-tau Yih, Greg Corrado, and Jeffrey Dean. 2013c. Linguistic Regularities in Continuous Space Word Representations. In *HLT-NAACL*.

[Řehůřek and Sojka2010] Radim Řehůřek and Petr Sojka. 2010. Software Framework for Topic Modelling with Large Corpora. In *Proceedings of the LREC 2010 Workshop on New Challenges for NLP Frameworks*, pages 45–50, Valletta, Malta, May. ELRA.

[Rosch and Mervis1975] Eleanor Rosch and Carolyn B Mervis. 1975. Family resemblances: Studies in the internal structure of categories. *Cognitive psychology*, 7(4):573–605.

[Schütze1993] Hinrich Schütze. 1993. Word space. In *Advances in Neural Information Processing Systems 5*.

[Turney2012] Peter Turney. 2012. Domain and Function: A Dual-Space Model of Semantic Relations and Compositions. *Journal of Artificial Intelligence Research*, pages 533–585.

[Veale and Hao2007] Tony Veale and Yanfen Hao. 2007. Comprehending and generating apt metaphors: a web-driven, case-based approach to figurative language. In *AAAI*, volume 2007, pages 1471–1476.

[Veale and Hao2008] Tony Veale and Yanfen Hao. 2008. A fluid knowledge representation for understanding and generating creative metaphors. In *Proceedings of the 22nd International Conference on Computational Linguistics-Volume 1*, pages 945–952. Association for Computational Linguistics.

[Veale et al.2000] Tony Veale, Diarmuid O Donoghue, and Mark T. Keane. 2000. Computation and blending. *Cognitive Linguistics*, 11(3/4):253–282.

[Veale2013] Tony Veale. 2013. Less rhyme, more reason: Knowledge-based poetry generation with feeling, insight and wit. In *Proceedings of the International Conference on Computational Creativity*, pages 152–159.

[WordNet2010] WordNet. 2010. Princeton University. http://wordnet.princeton.edu.

Gender-Distinguishing Features in Film Dialogue

Alexandra Schofield & Leo Mehr
Cornell University
Ithaca, NY 14850

Abstract

Film scripts provide a means of examining generalized western social perceptions of accepted human behavior. In particular, we focus on how dialogue in films describes gender, identifying linguistic and structural differences in speech for men and women and in same and different-gendered pairs. Using the Cornell Movie-Dialogs Corpus (Danescu-Niculescu-Mizil et al., 2012a), we identify significant linguistic and structural features of dialogue that differentiate genders in conversation and analyze how those effects relate to existing literature on gender in film.

1 Introduction

Film characterizations often rely on archetypes as shorthand to conserve narrative space. This effect comes out strongly when examining gender representations in films: assumptions about stereotypical gender roles can help establish expectations for characters and tension. It is also worth examining whether the gendered behavior in film reflects known language differences across gender lines, such as women's tendency towards speaking less or more politely (Lakoff, 1973), or the phenomenon of "troubles talk," a ritual in which women build relationships through talking about frustrating experiences or problems in their lives (Jefferson, 1988) in contrast to a more male process of using language primarily as a means of retaining status and attention (Tannen, 1991). We look at a large sample of scripts from well-known films to try to better understand how features of conversation vary with character gender.

We begin by examining utterances made by individual characters across a film, focusing on the classification task of identifying whether a speaker is male or female. We hypothesize that in film, speech between the two gender classes differs significantly. We isolate interesting lexical and structural features from the language models associated with male and female speech, subdividing to examine particular film genres to evaluate whether features are systematically different across all genres or whether distinguishing features differ on a per-genre basis.

We then focus on the text of conversations between two characters to identify whether the two speakers are both male, both female, or of opposite genders. One belief about gendered conversation expressed in films is that women and men act fundamentally differently around each other than around people of the same gender, due partly to differences in the function of speech as perceived by men and women (Tannen, 1991). We look into features that explore the hypothesis that there are significant differences in how men and women speak to each other that are not accounted for merely by the combination of a male and a female language model, and find distinguishing features in each of these three classes of language. Finally, we look at whether these conversation features have predictive power on the duration of a relationship in a film.

2 Data Description

Our dataset comes from the Cornell Movie-Dialogs Corpus (Danescu-Niculescu-Mizil et al., 2012a), a collection of dialogues from 617 film scripts. Of the characters in the corpus, 3015 have pre-existing gender labels. We obtain another 1358 gender labels for the remaining characters by taking the top 1000 US baby names for boys and girls and treating any character whose first listed name is on only one of these two lists as having the respective gender

Proceedings of the Fifth Workshop on Computational Linguistics for Literature, NAACL-HLT 2016, pages 32–39,
San Diego, California, June 1, 2016. ©2016 Association for Computational Linguistics

of the list. Based on hand-verification of a sample of 100 these newly-added labels, we achieved 94% labeling accuracy, implying that the 4373 character labels have about 98% accuracy. In practice, many of the mislabeled names seem to be from characters named for their job title or last name, suggesting that these characters have fairly little contribution to the dialogue. We investigated using IMDb data as an additional resource but discovered that variations in character naming make this task complex.

Women are less prominent than men across all films, both possessing fewer roles (30% of all roles in major films in 2014) and a smaller proportion of lead roles within them (Lauzen, 2015). This observation is matched quite well in the Movie-Dialogs corpus, where after supplementing gender labels, only 33.1% of characters are female (previously, 32.0% of the original characters were female). In addition, we record 4676 unique relationships (judged by having one or more conversations) with known character genders. A chi-squared test to compare the expected distribution of gender pairs from our character set to the actual relationships shows that the characters are not intermingling independently of gender ($p < 10^{-5}$), with only 374 of the expected 509 relationships between women and 2225 interactions between men compared to the expected 2099.

Subdividing our data further, we find that certain film genres as represented in this dataset have disproportionate representation of certain gender pairs with respect to gender. Table 1 shows the significant differences within genders of actual vs. expected number of characters and relationships of each gender type. Though we hypothesized that the gender gap may have narrowed over time, we find the gender ratio fairly consistent across time in our corpus, as shown in Figure 1.

3 Methods

3.1 Feature Engineering

Our text processing uses the Natural Language Toolkit (NLTK) (Bird et al., 2009). We use a simple tokenizer in our analysis that treats any sequence of alphanumerics as a word for our classifiers, splitting on punctuation and whitespace characters. We elect not to stem or remove stopwords, as non-contentful variation in language is important for our analysis.

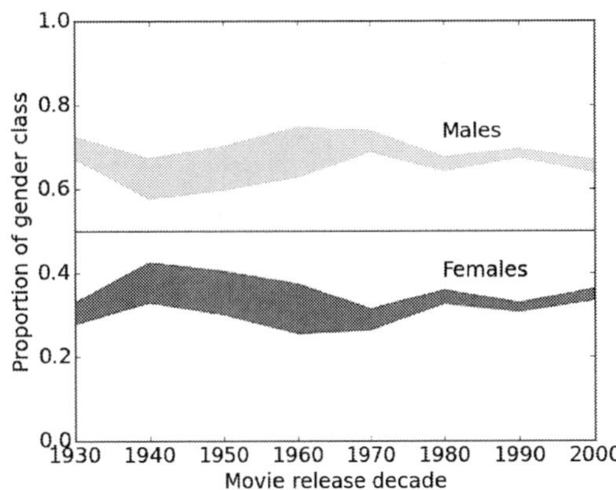

Figure 1: Proportion of character gender representation in movies, bucketed by decade, shaded by standard error.

Category	Key	Features
Lexical	LEX	unigrams, bigrams, trigrams
Vader Sentiment Scores	VADER	VADER scores for positive, negative, neutral, and composite value
Valence, Arousal, and Dominance	V/A/D	average scores across scored words
Structural	STR	average tokens per line, average token length, type to token ratio
Discourse	DIS	Δ average tokens per line, Δ average token length, Δ type to token ratio, unigram similarity

Table 2: List of feature groups. Δ indicates the absolute, unsigned difference between the text for each speaker. We discarded LEX features that arose fewer than 5 times.

Based on theory that women will have more hedging (Lakoff, 1973), we hypothesized that strength of sentiment or signals of arousal or dominance might also signal gender differences in convesation. We used sentiment labels from VADER (Hutto and Gilbert, 2014) and a list of 13,915 English words with scores describing valence, arousal, and dominance (Warriner et al., 2013). We group these features and several nonlexical discourse features into several primary groups, described in Table 2. We also experimented with part-of-speech labels using the Stanford POS tagger (Toutanova et al., 2003), but found they do not significantly influence results.

Genre	M	F		MM	FM	FF	
action	735	295	**	562	434	40	****
adventure	486	184	**	388	284	17	****
animation	82	34		68	41	5	
biography	156	63		128	80	13	
comedy	857	430		695	636	147	
crime	750	299	**	604	427	68	**
drama	1645	830		1278	1192	195	****
family	74	40		43	62	9	
fantasy	314	158		246	232	42	
history	95	42		80	46	5	**
horror	365	245	***	209	338	89	*
music	67	35		62	48	4	**
mystery	496	243		403	364	63	**
romance	660	372	*	463	566	119	*
sci-fi	502	205	*	381	321	27	****
thriller	1240	575		918	810	133	***
war	114	29	**	99	48	3	
western	79	40		66	51	12	

Table 1: Chi-squared test results on number of characters of each gender and number of gender relationship pairs given gender proportions. The character gender test is done in comparison to the 33% female baseline expectation for that number of characters, whereas the gender-pairs are with respect to the expected proportion of gender pairs were one to randomly draw two characters for each of the relationships observed. Only genres with more than 100 observed characters with assigned gender were included. Stars mark significance levels of p=0.05*, 0.01**, 0.001***, and 0.0001****.

We surveyed several types of simple classifiers in our prediction tasks: Gaussian and Multinomial Naive Bayes, and Logistic Regression. These implementations came from the **scikit-learn** Python library (Pedregosa et al., 2011).

3.2 Controlling Data

In comparing the language of males and females, we want to ensure that confounding factors do not result in significant results; the classification tasks should not yield better/worse results because of the structure of our dataset or the data we used to train/test. The first essential measure we take is to select equal numbers of males and females from each movie. Second, we only further select characters that have non-trivial amount of speech in the film. When selecting characters for single-speaker analysis, we use only those which had at least 3 conversations with other characters, 10 utterances, and 100 words spoken in total. This removes 45% of the characters from the original dataset. While the specific numbers are arbitrary, they were roughly selected after examining random character dialogs by hand. Third, we control for the language of a given movie or the style of its screenwriter(s) by using a leave-one-label-out split when running our classifiers.

Similarly for conversations, we control for each of the gender classes (male-male, female-male, and female-female), by including from each film the same number of conversations from each class. This results in a set of roughly 3500 conversations for consideration, a substantial subset of the original corpus but one with representation of a variety of dialogue lengths and less affected by the gender variation within particular films, to avoid classifying film content.

4 Experiments

4.1 Evaluating Individual Gender Features

We first examine the language differences in male and female utterances, selecting an equal number k_i of random male and female characters from each movie i. We then develop language models based upon the unigram, bigram, and trigram frequencies across all utterances from selected male characters versus female characters. As our focus is on usage of common words, we use raw term frequency instead of boolean features or TF-IDF weighting. While this does not fully control for the amount of speech of a given gender, it does control for variation in gender ratios and conversation subjects within films and genres.

We analyze the interesting n-grams using the weighted log-odds ratio metric with an informative Dirichlet prior (Monroe et al., 2008), distinguishing the significant tokens based upon single-tailed z-scores. Notably, with a large vocabulary, it is expected that some terms will randomly have large z-scores. We therefore only highlight n-grams with z-scores of greater magnitude than what arose in 19 out of 20 tests of random reshufflings of the lines of dialogue between gender classes (equivalent to the 95% certainty level of what is significant). The important n-grams are displayed in Figure 2.

The findings here conform to findings we would expect, such as cursing as a male-favored practice (Cressman et al., 2009) and polite words like greetings and "please" as more favored by women (Holmes, 2013). Interesting as well is the predominance of references to women in men's speech and men in women's speech: "she" and "her" are strongly favored by male speakers, while "he" and "him" are strongly favored by female speakers ($p <$ 0.00001). We also observe that in contrast to men's cursing, adverbial emphatics like "so", and "really" are favored by women, conforming to classic hypothesis about gendered language in the real world (Pennebaker et al., 2003; Lakoff, 1973).

4.2 Predicting Speaker Gender

Given only the words a character has spoken in conversations over the course of the movie, can we accurately predict the character gender?

As outlined in Controlling Data, we select characters equitably from each movie, each having spoken a significant amount during the movie. Using this method, we obtain 552 male and female characters each. We extract features from the all the lines spoken by each of these characters (as outlined in Feature Engineering), and train/test various scikit-learn built-in classifiers (as from Classifiers) in 10-fold cross-validation. As surveyed here, using a Logistic Regression classifier with different features, we obtain 72.2% classification accuracy (per feature accuracy outlined in Table 3). A multinomial Naive Bayes classifier performs slightly better, on which we applied the more appropriate leave-

one-label-out cross-validation method to split training and test data, at **73.6%**.

Features	Accuracy±Std. Error
Baseline	50.0±0.3%
STR	55.2±2.1%
Unigrams	67.4±1.7%
LEX	**71.7±1.9%**
LEX + STR	**72.0±1.9%**
LEX + STR + VADER	**72.2±1.2%**

Table 3: Performance of single-speaker gender classification. Bolded outcomes are those statistically insignificantly different from the best result (using a two-tailed z-test).

4.3 Evaluating Relationship Text

While the previous section demonstrates systemic differences in language between male and female speakers, an additional factor to consider is the conversation participants of each of these dialogues. We can hypothesize that, in addition to having different lexical content between men and women, movies also demonstrate significant content differences between pairs of interacting genders, such that the conversation patterns of men and women talking to each other have different content than same-gendered conversations.

We can examine this hypothesis by repeating the analysis performed on single characters throughout a film on individual conversations from films. We use the controlled dataset described in the Methods section, this time contrasting each class of gender pair: male-male, female-male, and female-female (MM, FM, and FF, respectively). We include the most significant words in each class in Table 4. As with the single-gender analysis, we see that men seem to speak about women with other men, and women about men with other women. We also note that several pronouns including "she" and "he" from before are actually considered statistically less probable in two-gendered conversations.

This is an interesting signal of men speaking differently around men than around women, which, in conjunction with the high log-odds ratio of "feel", "you", and "you love" favoring dual-gendered conversations, suggests that men and women are more likely to be talking about feelings and each other, while they are more likely to talk about experiences

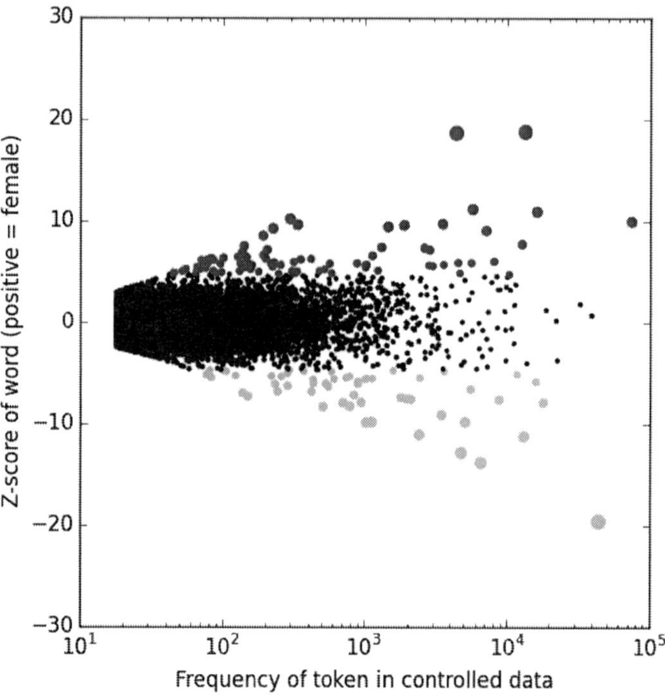

Figure 2: Tokens with significance plotted with respect to log-odds ratio. We ran 20 randomization trials and found that in those trials, the largest magnitude z-score we saw was 4.7. Blue labels at the top refer to female words above that significance magnitude, while orange labels at the bottom refer to words below that significance.

of the other-gendered people in their lives with their same-gendered friends. While this finding does not fully support that women and men are not friends in films, it does suggest the idea that men and women in films are typically interacting in a way distinct from men and women without consideration of context. It also contrasts with the typical understanding of sharing personal problems as a female practice (Tannen, 1991), as it seems that both men and women in films use words discussing feelings and people of the other gender.

4.4 Predicting Gender Pairs

In order to focus on the linguistic differences of the content of conversations between our gender pair classes instead of the success of per-character gender classifiers, we took as our additional classification task the problem of predicting the gender pair of the speakers in a conversation. This task is considerably more difficult than most, as conversa-tions are often short and will include multiple speakers. We again use leave-one-label-out training to avoid learning dialogue cues from movies. While we can again attain better accuracy with a multinomial Naive Bayes classifier on LEX features, for our objective of simply demonstrating that features provide indication of gender differences, we are satisfied to use logistic regression to incorporate all features.

As Table 5 shows, the only features producing significant improvement over a random accuracy baseline of 33% are lexical, structural, and discourse features. While the fact that lexical content has distinguishing power is perhaps unsurprising, given the preceding analysis, it is somewhat more surprising that more simple structural and discourse features are also producing significant results.

While there no obvious significant structural differences, one can spot minor variation that seems to provide the slight improvement above random in our classification in Figure 3. We observe in Figure 3a

MM		FM		FF	
n-gram	z	n-gram	z	n-gram	z
her	8.2	feel	3.9	he s	9.0
she	7.7	you	3.5	he	7.2
the	7.0	you love	3.0	him	6.3
man	6.7	walk	2.8	he was	4.6
this	4.6	happy	2.8	dear	4.2
sir	4.3	tough	2.8	honey	4.0
you	-3.6	in my	-2.6	up	-3.4
honey	-3.8	every	-2.8	man	-3.8
him	-4.4	man	-3.1	her	-4.3
love	-4.8	she	-3.4	she	-4.5
he	-4.8	he	-4.2	mr	-4.5
hes	-4.9	her	-4.2	the	-5.2

Table 4: The six top words and z-scores correlated with the topic positively and negatively when comparing log-odds ratios for each gender class with respect to the other two. While a z-score of magnitude 2.8 has a significance of $p < 0.003$, the size of the considered vocabulary makes it unsurprising that several words have scores of this magnitude randomly; however, in twenty trials of randomization of the text between classes, only one z-scores emerged greater than magnitude 3.1. We therefore infer z-scores higher than 3.1 or lower than -3.1 are unlikely to be the consequence of random variation between classes.

that while utterance length is significantly higher for all-male than all-female conversations, two-gender conversations seem to behave more like all-female conversations on average. Figure 3b looks again at speaker utterances in combination with their imbalance between speakers, the "delta" average utterance length. Our comparison shows a significant difference between men talking to men and men talking to women. As delta utterance length here explicitly is described by average female utterance length minus average male utterance length, this demonstrates that women are speaking in shorter utterances than men in male-female conversations, in contrast to having longer utterances overall. Word length also is significantly shorter for women than men in single-gender conversations, but in this case, the two-gendered value appears to be just the interpolation of the two single-gender values, suggesting that word length is not decreased for male characters in two-gender conversation.

We also can see some interesting discourse features in Figure 3c. While looking at the data confirms that the average type-to-token ratio does not

Features	Accuracy±Std. Error
LEX	**38±1%**
VADER	33±1%
V/A/D	35±1%
STR + DIS	**37±1%**
LEX + STR + DIS	**37±1%**
All but LEX	35±1%
All	**38±1%**

Table 5: Classifier results using logistic regression on the features from Table 2. Lexical features are sufficient to produce nonrandom classification, as well as structural and discourse features. Bolded text indicates a result better than random ($p < 0.05$).

differ between our three conversation classes, we find that the type-token ratio difference is significantly higher for conversations between two genders, which suggests that two-gender conversations may have an increased probability of demonstrating one character as less articulate than another. Looking into the data, this slightly but insignificantly favors women having a higher type-to-token ratio than men, suggesting they use more unique words in their speech than do men in conversation. Finally, we note that conversations with women have significantly higher unigram similarity than men. This hints there may be some linguistic mirroring effect that women in film demonstrate more than men, which may relate to the hypothesis that women coordinate language more to build relationships (Danescu-Niculescu-Mizil et al., 2012b; Tannen, 1991).

4.5 Relationship Prediction

In addition to testing the prediction of genders in conversations and relationships, we attempted to use the same features to distinguish from a single conversation whether a relationship would be short (3 or fewer conversations) or long (more than 3 conversations). We tested on a dataset of conversations split evenly between gender pairs and between long and short relationships, using leave-one-label-out cross validation to test conversations from one relationship at a time. With a multinomial Naive Bayes classifier, we are able to achieve $60 \pm 2\%$ accuracy with a combination of n-gram features, gender labels, and structural and discourse features. Performing ablation with each feature set used, we find that results worsen by omitting either structural features ($54 \pm 2\%$) or n-gram features ($54 \pm 2\%$), but that omitting gender from the classification does

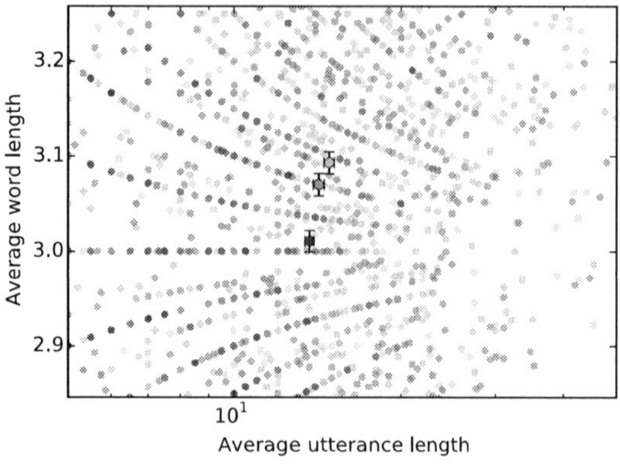

(a) Structural features.

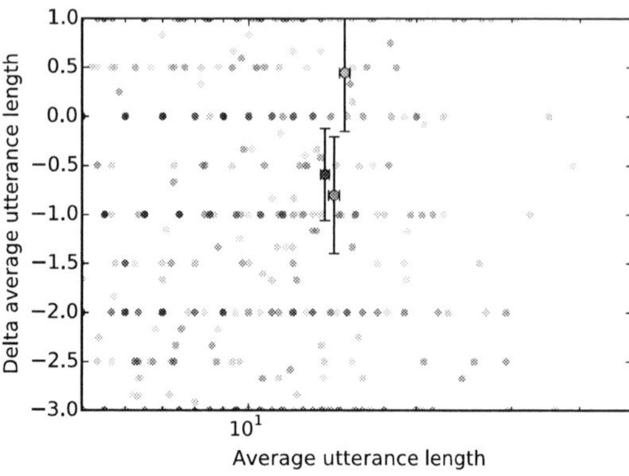

(b) Utterance length.

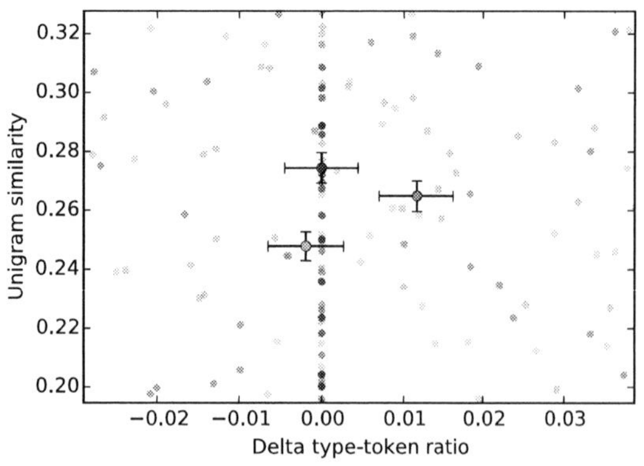

(c) Discourse features.

Figure 3: Structural and discourse features plotted with respect to each other, focusing on the region of means (circled in black). Orange and blue refer to male-male and female-female conversations, while pink refers to two-gender conversations. Standard errors for both axes are plotted in each figure but are sometimes too small to distinguish.

not significantly impact the classification accuracy ($60 \pm 2\%$).

Some of this result is predictable from the limits of the data: controlling for the number of conversations in a relationship heavily limits the number of possible short female relationships. Our dataset has few labels for minor female roles and thus short, explicitly female-female relationships are hard to find. In addition, though, analysis of the lexical features that predict this suggest that the difference is fairly subtle, more so than a gender divide might suggest: the significant positive indicators of a long relationship with respect to randomly significant are "it," "we," and "we ll", while the negative indicators are "name," "he," and "mr," which suggest that the identification of a collective "we" might show a longer connection but very little else that obviously signals a relationship's length.

5   Related Work

There exists prior work analyzing the differences in language between male and female writing, by Argamon, Koppel, Fine, and Shimoni (Argamon et al., 2003). Herring and Paolillo at Indiana University have shown relations in the style and content of weblogs to the gender of the writer (Herring and Paolillo, 2006). The investigative strategy we use for comparing n-gram probabilities stems from work done by Monroe, Colaresi, and Quinn on distinguishing the contentful differences in language of conservatives and liberals on political subjects (Monroe et al., 2008). Recently, researchers used a simpler version of n-gram analysis to distinguish funded from not-funded Kickstarter campaigns based on linguistic cues (Mitra and Gilbert, 2014).

6   Conclusion

Finding words that are stereotypically male or female came can be done rather quickly and roughly. Yet more sophisticated techniques provide more reliable and believable data. Isolating the right subset of the data to use with proper control methods, and then extracting useful information from this subset results in interesting and significant results. In our small dataset, we find that simple lexical features were by far the most useful for prediction, and that sentiment and structure prove less effective in the setting of our movie scripts corpus. We also isolate several simpler discourse features that suggest interesting differences between single-gender and two-gender conversations and gendered speech.

7 Acknowledgements

We thank C. Danescu-Niculescu-Mizil, L. Lee, D. Mimno, J. Hessel, and the members of the NLP and Social Interaction course at Cornell for their support and ideas in developing this paper. We thank the workshop chairs and our anonymous reviewers for their thoughtful comments and suggestions.

References

[Argamon et al.2003] Shlomo Argamon, Moshe Koppel, Jonathan Fine, and Anat Rachel Shimoni. 2003. Gender, genre, and writing style in formal written texts. *Text & Talk*, 23(3):321–346.

[Bird et al.2009] Steven Bird, Ewan Klein, and Edward Loper. 2009. *Natural language processing with Python*. O'Reilly Media. Available at http://www.nltk.org/book/.

[Cressman et al.2009] Dale L Cressman, Mark Callister, Tom Robinson, and Chris Near. 2009. Swearing in the cinema: An analysis of profanity in US teen-oriented movies, 1980–2006. *Journal of Children and Media*, 3(2):117–135.

[Danescu-Niculescu-Mizil et al.2012a] Cristian Danescu-Niculescu-Mizil, Justin Cheng, Jon Kleinberg, and Lillian Lee. 2012a. You had me at hello: How phrasing affects memorability. In *Proceedings of ACL*, pages 892–901.

[Danescu-Niculescu-Mizil et al.2012b] Cristian Danescu-Niculescu-Mizil, Lillian Lee, Bo Pang, and Jon Kleinberg. 2012b. Echoes of power: Language effects and power differences in social interaction. In *Proceedings of the 21st international conference on World Wide Web*, pages 699–708. ACM.

[Herring and Paolillo2006] Susan C Herring and John C Paolillo. 2006. Gender and genre variation in weblogs. *Journal of Sociolinguistics*, 10(4):439–459.

[Holmes2013] Janet Holmes. 2013. *Women, men and politeness*. Routledge.

[Hutto and Gilbert2014] CJ Hutto and Eric Gilbert. 2014. Vader: A parsimonious rule-based model for sentiment analysis of social media text. In *Eighth International AAAI Conference on Weblogs and Social Media*.

[Jefferson1988] Gail Jefferson. 1988. On the sequential organization of troubles-talk in ordinary conversation. *Social problems*, 35(4):418–441.

[Lakoff1973] Robin Lakoff. 1973. Language and woman's place. *Language in society*, 2(01):45–79.

[Lauzen2015] Martha M Lauzen. 2015. It's a man's (celluloid) world: On-screen representations of female characters in the top 100 films of 2014. Center for the Study of Women in Television and Film, http://womenintvfilm.sdsu.edu/files/2014_Its_a_Mans_World_Report.pdf.

[Mitra and Gilbert2014] Tanushree Mitra and Eric Gilbert. 2014. The language that gets people to give: Phrases that predict success on kickstarter. In *Proceedings of the 17th ACM conference on computer supported cooperative work & social computing*, pages 49–61. ACM.

[Monroe et al.2008] Burt L Monroe, Michael P Colaresi, and Kevin M Quinn. 2008. Fightin'words: Lexical feature selection and evaluation for identifying the content of political conflict. *Political Analysis*, 16(4):372–403.

[Pedregosa et al.2011] F. Pedregosa, G. Varoquaux, A. Gramfort, V. Michel, B. Thirion, O. Grisel, M. Blondel, P. Prettenhofer, R. Weiss, V. Dubourg, J. Vanderplas, A. Passos, D. Cournapeau, M. Brucher, M. Perrot, and E. Duchesnay. 2011. Scikit-learn: Machine learning in Python. *Journal of Machine Learning Research*, 12:2825–2830.

[Pennebaker et al.2003] James W Pennebaker, Matthias R Mehl, and Kate G Niederhoffer. 2003. Psychological aspects of natural language use: Our words, our selves. *Annual review of psychology*, 54(1):547–577.

[Tannen1991] Deborah Tannen. 1991. *You just don't understand: Women and men in conversation*. Virago London.

[Toutanova et al.2003] Kristina Toutanova, Dan Klein, Christopher D Manning, and Yoram Singer. 2003. Feature-rich part-of-speech tagging with a cyclic dependency network. In *Proceedings of the 2003 Conference of the North American Chapter of the ACL on Human Language Technology-Volume 1*, pages 173–180. ACL.

[Warriner et al.2013] Amy Beth Warriner, Victor Kuperman, and Marc Brysbaert. 2013. Norms of valence, arousal, and dominance for 13,915 English lemmas. *Behavior research methods*, 45(4):1191–1207.

Reconstructing Ancient Literary Texts from Noisy Manuscripts

Moshe Koppel
Dept. of Computer Science,
Bar Ilan University
Ramat-Gan, Israel

moishk@gmail.com

Moty Michaely
Dept. of Computer Science,
Bar Ilan University
Ramat-Gan, Israel

moty.mi@gmail.com

Alex Tal
Dept. of Jewish Thought,
University of Haifa
Haifa, Israel

msaltal@gmail.com

Abstract

Given multiple corrupted versions of the same text, as is common with ancient manuscripts, we wish to reconstruct the original text from which the extant corrupted versions were copied (typically via latent intermediary versions). This is a challenge of cardinal importance in the humanities. We use a variant of expectation-maximization (EM), to solve this problem. We prove the efficacy of our method on both synthetic and real-world data.

1 Introduction

In ancient times, original documents were written by hand and then copied by scribes. Some societies transmitted traditions orally, which were written down and copied at some later date. These copies were inevitably inexact, each scribe introducing some errors into the text. These flawed copies spread around the world where they were then themselves imperfectly copied. Some small subset of these repeatedly corrupted documents survived until modern times.

One of the main tasks of the study of such ancient manuscripts is to reconstruct the original document (the "ur-text") from the corrupted manuscripts that are available. This has traditionally been done using painstaking manual methods. In this paper, we show this reconstruction can be au-

tomated using a variant of the expectation-maximization (EM) algorithm (Dempster et al 1977).

The structure of the paper is as follows. In the next section, we consider previous work on the ur-text problem (mostly dealing with a different version of the problem). In Section 3, we define the synoptic form in which we assume the texts are presented. In Sections 4 and 5, we formalize the problem and present our solution. In the three subsequent sections, we consider synthetic, artificial and real-world testbeds, respectively.

2 Previous Work

The reconstruction of ur-texts from corrupted manuscripts using manual methods has a long history (Maas 1958, West 1973). Such methods can be divided roughly into methods designed to select a single best manuscript (a "diplomatic" text) from among the extant ones (Bedier 1928) and methods designed to create an optimal hybrid (an "eclectic" text) out of the extant manuscripts (Lachmann 1853, Timpanaro 2005).

From a computational point of view, it is clear that the Bedierian approach is preferable when the collection of extant manuscripts for a given text is relatively complete (in the sense that the earlier manuscripts from which later manuscripts were copied are also included in the collection), especially if the ur-text itself might be found in the collection. In these cases, the main challenge is to re-

Proceedings of the Fifth Workshop on Computational Linguistics for Literature, NAACL-HLT 2016, pages 40–46,
San Diego, California, June 1, 2016. ©2016 Association for Computational Linguistics

construct the *stemma*, the tree that records which manuscript was copied from which. The root of the reconstructed stemma is hypothesized to be the ur-text.

This challenge is common with bio-informatics (Pupko et al. 2000, Yang 2007) and researchers have applied methods of bio-informatics to the reconstruction of document stemmata (Robinson and O'Hara 1996, Robinson et al. 1998, Roos and Heikkila 2009, Roelli and Bachmann 2010, Andrews and Mace 2013).

Hoenen (2015) considers the problem of automated ur-text reconstruction for cases in which the manuscript collection is relatively complete and compares several methods of post-processing reconstructed stemmata to obtain (possibly eclectic) hypothesized ur-texts.

In the case of ancient documents, which we consider in this paper, the situation in which a collection is relatively complete – and might even include the ur-text – is exceedingly rare. Typically, the available manuscripts might be identifiable as (near or distant) cousins, but will be too sparse to permit even partial stemma reconstruction. Thus, we will develop an entirely new approach that does not focus on stemma reconstruction, as previous work did.

Our approach involves three stages. First, all the manuscripts for a given text must be arranged so that parallel words or phrases are aligned in columns ("synoptic form"). Second, when possible, related manuscripts should be clustered together. Finally, the ur-text can be inferred from the aligned, clustered texts by using statistical methods to make the optimal choice in each column of the synoptic text.

3   Creating a Synopsis

Consider the simple synopsis shown in Figure 1.

United	States	on	the	4th	of	July
USA		on		Fourth	of	July
United	States	in	the	end	of	June

Figure 1: A fragment of a synoptic text.

As is evident even in this simple example, there are a number of subtleties involved in creating such synopses. First, phrases (or any sequence of words that are inter-dependent) should ideally be in a single column, so that columns are as independent of each other as possible. For example, the phrase "United States" (and the acronym "USA") should be in a single column. (As in this example, typical available synopses are not ideal in this sense.) Second, words that differ only in trivial orthographic ways that are not important to us ought to be conflated. For example, we might choose not to distinguish between "4th" and "Fourth". Finally, distinct words that play the same role in the text (fourth/end; June/July) should be aligned, though often this is a matter of judgment.

One important limitation of such synopses is their monotonicity: the words in each row are laid out in the order they are found in the corresponding manuscript. Thus, if some manuscript inverts the order of two strings of text, one of those strings will not correspond to its parallels in other rows.

There have been efforts to automate the process of creating synopses from raw text. One approach adapts alignment methods developed in bio-informatics for aligning strings of DNA (Notredame et al. 2002). However, since the "words" aligned in bio-informatics are chosen from a small alphabet, whereas the words in texts are chosen from a large lexicon, such adaptation is not straightforward. There also are alignment methods designed specifically for text alignment (Robinson 1989, Spencer and Howe 2004, Dekker et al. 2014), as well as methods for aligning parallel texts in multiple languages (Och and Ney 2003).

Existing methods for text alignment are adequate for our purposes. As it happens, for the testbeds considered in this paper, manual synopses were available, allowing us to focus on the more basic issue of ur-text reconstruction.

4   Formalizing the Problem

Suppose now that we have a synopsis of n manuscripts each of which makes some choice with regard to each of m words (tokens) each appearing in a different column. We can think of our synopsis as an m*n matrix $a = \{a_{ij}\}$, where a_{ij} is the word (form) in the jth column according to the ith manuscript. (Some of these words might be blanks, which we treat exactly like any other token.) Given such a synopsis, we wish to choose the most probable choice in each column. The resulting sequence of words is the proposed ur-text.

How can we determine the most probable choice in each column? A straightforward baseline solution is to use simple majority rule (SMR): for each column, choose the token found most frequently in that column. Under certain trivial conditions, Condorcet's Jury Theorem guarantees that this method's accuracy approaches 1 as the number of manuscripts grows.

In real-life, however, the number of manuscripts available is usually quite limited. We will introduce a method that yields considerably stronger results than SMR for the kinds of situations encountered in the real world.

We will assume that each manuscript i has some reliability level, p_i. This means that for any given token, manuscript i has probability p_i of choosing the right token (that is, using the same form that is being transcribed). Of course, the value p_i is not known to us. Our objective will be to show how to simultaneously find the most likely reliability levels of the respective manuscripts and the most likely ur-text.

Our initial generative model is as follows: a single ur-text of length m is copied by each of n scribes. For any token $j \in \{1,...,m\}$, there is probability p_i that the scribe of manuscript $i \in \{1,...,n\}$ will transcribe the token correctly. If he fails to transcribe a token correctly, there are k_j equiprobable potential distinct forms other than the original. (Note that the number of potential forms might be different for different tokens.) One limitation of this generative model is that we assume, perhaps unrealistically, that for any given scribe the probability of an error is the same for every word.

We do not assume that for all i, $p_i > .5$. Rather, for the binary case ($k_j=1$), we assume only the almost trivial condition that $\prod p_i > \prod (1-p_i)$; for non-binary cases, the necessary condition is even weaker. Note that for the binary case, the necessary condition is weaker in the limit than the necessary condition for Condorcet's Jury Theorem (Berend and Paroush 1998): $\lim_{n \to \infty} \text{average}(p_i-1/2)\sqrt{n} = \infty$.

Thus our synopsis $a=\{a_{ij}\}$ is such that each column has at most k_j+1 distinct choices: one correct choice and k_j equiprobable potential alternative forms. We arbitrarily map each choice to a number in the set $\{1,...,k_j+1\}$.

An ur-text reconstruction is a mapping from the synopsis $a=\{a_{ij}\}$ to a proposed text in $\{1,...,k_j+1\}^m$. Our objective is to find an optimal reconstruction, given no information other than the synopsis $a = \{a_{ij}\}$.

5   Our Proposed Method

We treat our problem as an instance of judgment aggregation in which each of a set of judges (manuscripts) makes judgments regarding multiple issues (words). This problem has been handled (Baharad et al 2011, Bachrach et al 2012, Hovy et al. 2013) using variants of EM; we adapt this approach here for our purposes.

In principle, given the set of scribal reliabilities $\{p_i\}_i$ and the probabilities in each column of each distinct form being the correct (original) form, $\{p(t_j=w|w \in \{1,...,k_j+1\})\}_j$ (or for short, $\{p(t_j=w)\}_j$) we could compute the conditional probability of obtaining the synopsis a. Thus, given some synopsis a, optimality is obtained by the values of $\{p_i\}_i$ and $\{p(t_j=w)\}_j$ that maximize the likelihood of a. As shown below, the values $\{p(t_j=w)\}_j$ can be determined from a and $\{p_i\}_i$. Thus, denoting by $p(a;\{p_i\})$ the likelihood of a given the parameters $\{p_i\}_i$, our objective is to maximize $p(a;\{p_i\})$.

Our algorithm, which we'll call UR, finds a local maximum for $p(a;\{p_i\})$ as follows. First, for each token j, we estimate the value of k_j by simply assuming that every distinct form with non-zero probability actually occurs in one of the manuscripts (i.e., k_j is one less than the number of distinct forms that appear in the column). Clearly, this estimate is only plausible when the number of manuscripts is large, but we find that it is good enough for our purposes.

We assign some initial constant value to $\{p_i\}_i$. Then we repeat the following two steps until convergence:

1. Use the manuscript reliabilities $\{p_i\}_i$ to recompute the values $\{p(t_j=w)\}_j$.

2. Use the values $\{p(t_j=w)\}_j$ to estimate the maximum likelihood values of the manuscript reliabilities $\{p_i\}_i$.

For the first step, we assume that for every j the prior $\{p(t_j=w)$ is equal for every $w \in \{1,...,k_j+1\}$.

Then we have by Bayes' rule that for each j and each $w \in \{1,\ldots,k_j+1\}$,

$$p(t_j{=}\mathrm{w}\mid a) = p(t_j{=}\mathrm{w}\mid a_j) = \frac{p(a_j \mid t_j{=}w)}{Z}$$

where a_j is the jth column of a and Z is a normalization factor. This can easily be computed by substituting

$$p(a_j \mid t_j{=}\mathrm{w}) = \prod_{a_{ij}=\mathrm{w}} p_i * \prod_{a_{ij}\neq\mathrm{w}}(1{-}p_i)/k_j \ .$$

For the second step, we compare the values $\{p(t_j{=}\mathrm{w})\}_j$ to the judgments of individual i, in order to compute the maximum-likelihood values of $\{p_i\}_i$. Specifically, the maximum likelihood value of p_i is equal to the average (over j) probability that $a_{ij} = t_j$. Thus, our updated value of $p_i = \frac{1}{m}\left(\sum_j p(t_j = a_{ij}\mid a)\right)$.

It can be shown that the method converges to a local maximum of $p(a;\{p_i\})$.

5.1 Handling Dependencies

The above method would guarantee a (locally) optimal solution if it were the case that manuscripts are independent of each other. In fact, however, manuscripts are copied from one another, so that various extant manuscripts might have some common ancestor (subsequent to the ur-text). Thus, for example, third-generation manuscripts fall naturally into clusters, reflecting the second-order manuscript from which they are copied. The errors in manuscripts in the same cluster tend to be similar.

Even when, as is usually the case, we don't have a sufficiently complete collection of manuscripts to reconstruct a stemma, we might have enough (possibly external) information to at least divide the collection into several flat clusters of related manuscripts. Given such a clustering, we can use the UR method to identify the ur-text for each cluster and then use UR once again to reconstruct the original ur-text from the multiple second-generation ur-texts.

In most real life cases, domain experts are able to identify flat clusters (but not a full stemma) using external evidence. In cases where the clusters are not known, automatic clustering methods must be used to identify them.

6 Experiments – Synthetic Synopses

6.1 Direct Transcription

We first test our method on synthetic manuscripts. For our initial experiment, we assume that there is a single ur-text T consisting of m words. T is copied directly by each of n scribes. (In these experiments, we use n=20.) Each manuscript is assigned some random reliability p_i (the probability of copying a given word correctly) chosen from a uniform distribution between 0.20 and 0.99. In addition, for each word w_j, we let k_j have equal chances of being either 1 or 2. If a word is copied incorrectly, it is randomly replaced by one of k_j possible other words.

For each trial, we use the method described above to reconstruct the ur-text. As a baseline method, we use simple majority rule (SMR) to decide which word to choose in each column of the synopsis.

We run 1000 trials as described above, showing results for different manuscript lengths. For each algorithm in each trial, we check the proportion of words that are reconstructed correctly and we average the results over all trials. In Figure 2, we show the results.

UR improves initially as manuscript length increases since its estimates of manuscript reliability improve, while SMR is indifferent to manuscript length.

In Figure 3, we show results for the same setup where document length is fixed at 100 but the number of manuscripts varies. UR clearly outperforms the baseline simple majority rule.

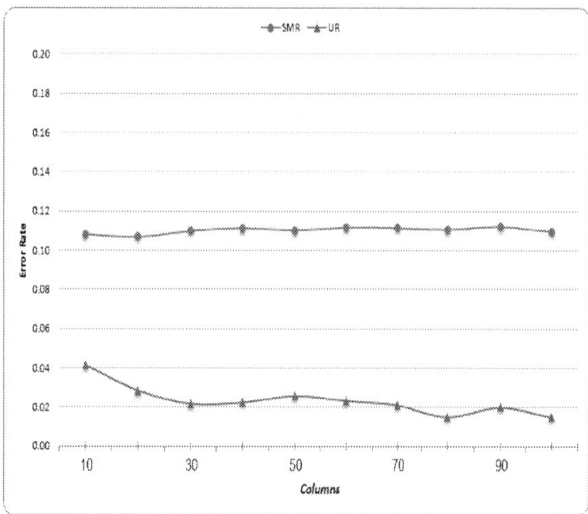

Figure 2: Word error rate in reconstruction using UR and SMR, respectively, for varying manuscript lengths.

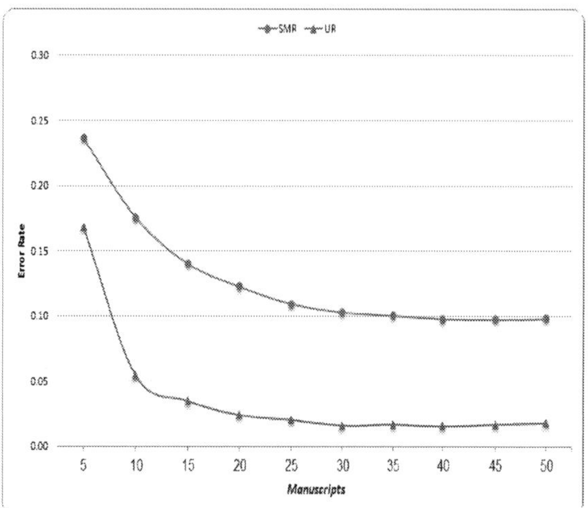

Figure 3: Word error rate in reconstruction using UR and SMR, respectively, for varying numbers of manuscripts.

6.2   Latent Manuscripts

For our next set of experiments, we drop the assumption that all extant manuscripts are copied directly from the ur-text. Instead, we assume that our manuscripts are copies of copies. We generate 20 second-generation manuscripts by noisily copying the ur-text T 20 times, exactly as above. Now we generate 200 third-generation manuscripts, each time randomly choosing one of the second-generation manuscripts and copying it noisily according to some randomly-chosen reliability (from the same distribution as above). These 200 third-generation manuscripts serve as input.

We call the second-generation manuscripts to which we do not have access "latent" manuscripts and we call the set of third-generation manuscripts that are generated from a given second-generation manuscript a "cluster". In these experiments, we assume that the clusters are known.

For each trial, we use each of the following algorithms for regenerating the ur-text:

1. SMR
2. UR
3. Recursive SMR
4. Recursive UR

The recursive methods run the algorithm on each cluster separately and then again on the results of the respective clusters.

In Figure 4, we show accuracy results averaged over 1000 trials as described above, showing results for different manuscript lengths. We find that UR that ignores clustering performs very poorly but Recursive UR is much stronger, outperforming both versions of SMR. (For all data-points, standard error is <.005, too small to be seen.)

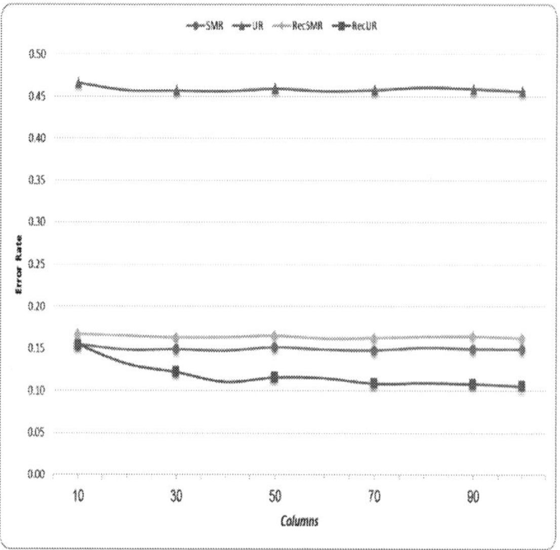

Figure 4: Word error rate in reconstruction using UR and SMR, respectively, for varying manuscript lengths, with and without clustering of manuscripts.

7   An Artificial Manuscript Testbed

As noted above, our method is appropriate for cases in which only a fraction of the manuscripts in the stemma are extant. In cases where the bulk of the stemma – possibly including the ur-text itself –

is extant, it would be better to attempt to reconstruct the stemma and identify the actual ur-text.

Notre Besoin (Baret et al 2006) is an artificial
collection of manuscripts generated by having
"scribes" successively copy an Old French manuscript. Thirteen manuscripts of length 1020 were
generated in this fashion. The full set of manuscripts (including the ur-text itself) was used as a
basis for comparing several methods for stemma
reconstruction (Roos and Heikkila 2009) and ur-
text reconstruction (Hoenen 2014).

Although this is a situation in which we regard
our method as less appropriate than stemma reconstruction methods, we run it for comparison purposes.

Hoenen found that an automated method
(PAML) for stemma reconstruction (Yang 2007),
yields an ur-text with word error rate of 4.7% and
that post-processing the obtained stemma using a
method akin to Recursive SMR lowers the word
error rate to 4.1%. We find that applying Recursive
UR to three non-hierarchical clusters – the de-
scendants of the three highest-level non-root nodes
in the stemma reconstructed by PAML (provided
by A. Hoenen) – while ignoring all other information in the stemma, yields an ur-text word error
rate of 4.6%. Thus the complete stemma reconstruction offers no clear benefit beyond the shallow
clustering method for our purposes.

8   A Real-World Manuscript Testbed

Finally, we consider a real-world example. The
Babylonian Talmud is a 6th century Aramaic com-
pendium transmitted orally and written down several centuries later in Hebrew letters in Iraq. We
use a synoptic version of a single chapter of the
Talmud (the second chapter of Tractate Beitzah),
consisting of 8564 columns and 20 manuscripts,
seven of which are relatively complete and the rest
of which are very fragmentary. A domain expert
established that, based on external evidence, the
manuscripts split naturally into six identifiable
clusters (containing 8, 4, 3, 3, 1, and 1 manuscripts, respectively).

Several pre-processing steps are applied to the
raw synopsis. First, we automatically identify minor orthographic variants within a given column
and standardize them so that they are treated as
identical. Furthermore, since the raw synopsis includes single words, rather than phrases, in a given
column, there are many dependencies among consecutive columns. To eliminate the most egregious
such dependencies, we iteratively conflate to a single column all perfectly correlated consecutive
columns. After conflating dependent columns in
this way, we remain with 5912 columns. In Figure
5, we show the proportion of these columns contain a single form, two variant forms, and so on. As
can be seen, only for 17% of the columns do all
manuscripts agree.

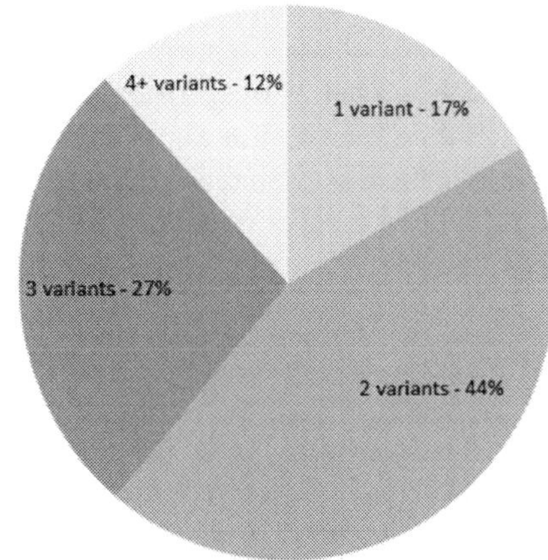

Figure 5: The proportion of columns in the Beitzah corpus
containing a given number of word forms

We apply Recursive UR, as well as Recursive
SMR as a baseline method, to the processed synopsis. Recursive UR assigns the six clusters reliabilities ranging from 0.46 to 0.78, with the highest
reliability assigned to a cluster consisting of a single manuscript indeed considered to be particularly
ancient and trustworthy.

The two methods disagree for 448 of the columns and agree for the rest. Our domain expert
(who did not know which word choice came from
which method) provided the most likely correct
word according to his own judgment for those columns for which the two methods disagree. Of the
448 disagreements, he determined that 80 were
significant and resolvable. In 66 of these 80 cases
(82.5%), the expert's judgment coincided with the
form chosen by UR and in only 14 cases (17.5%),
his judgment coincided with SMR.

9   Conclusions

We have found that ur-texts can be reconstructed using automated methods far more effectively than using a simple majority rule. Furthermore, this can be done to some extent even using only manuscripts from the third-generation and later.

We have assumed that the correct clustering of manuscripts is known. Left for future work is the case in which the clusters are identified using automated clustering methods.

More importantly, perhaps, we have assumed throughout that a given manuscript has some fixed reliability over all words. In fact, it might be the case that reliability varies over different tokens (or types) and that, moreover, not each distinct form of a word is an equally probable alternative to the original. Graphical models could be used to generalize our approach to handle such cases.

References

Andrews, TL and C. Mace. 2013. Beyond the tree of texts: Building an empirical model of scribal variation through graph analysis of texts and stemmas. *Literary and Linguistic Computing*, 28(4):504–521.

Bachrach, Y., T Graepel, T Minka, J Guiver (2012). How To Grade a Test Without Knowing the Answers-- A Bayesian Graphical Model for Adaptive Crowdsourcing and Aptitude Testing, *Proceedings of ICML.*

Baharad, E., Goldberger, J., Koppel, M. and Nitzan, S. (2011), Distilling the Wisdom of Crowds: Weighted Aggregation of Decisions on Multiple Issues, *JAAMAS* 22(1), 31-42.

Baret, P., Macé, C. and Robinson, P. (2006), Testing methods on an artificially created textual tradition, in C. Mace, P. Baret, A. Bozzi, L. Cignoni (eds.), *Linguistica Computazionale. The evolution of texts: confronting stemmato-logical and genetical methods*, XXIV-XXV, Pisa-Roma, Istituti Editoriali e Poligrafici Internazionali, pp. 255-283.

Bedier, J (1928). *La tradition manuscrite du 'Lai de l'Ombre': Reflexions sur l'Art d'Editer les Anciens Textes.* Romania, 394:161–196, 321–356.

Berend, Daniel and Paroush, Jacob (1998). When is Condorcet's Jury Theorem valid?. *Social Choice and Welfare* 15 (4)

Dekker, R., D. van Hulle, G. Middell, V. Neyt, J. van Zundert (2014). Computer-supported collation of modern manuscripts: CollateX and the Beckett Digital Manuscript Project, *LLC: Digital Scholarship in the Humanities* 25. 452-470

Dempster, A. P., N. M. Laird and D. B. Rubin (1977). Maximum Likelihood from Incomplete Data via the EM Algorithm, *Journal of the Royal Statistical Society.* Series B 39(1): 1-38.

Hoenen, A (2015). Lachmannian Archetype Reconstruction for Ancient Manuscript Corpora. *HLT-NAACL* 2015: 1209-1214

Hovy, D., Taylor Berg-Kirkpatrick, Ashish Vaswani, and Eduard Hovy (2013). Learning Whom to Trust with MACE. *Proceedings of NAACL-HLT* 2013

Lachmann, K (1853). *In T. Lucretii Cari De rerum natura libros commentarius.* Georg Reimer.

Maas, P. (1958). *Textual Criticism (tr. B. Flower)*, Oxford

Notredame, C. (2002) Recent progress in multiple sequence alignment: a survey. *Pharmacogenomics*, 3, 131–144.

Och, F. and Ney, H. (2003). A systematic comparison of various statistical alignment models. *Computational Linguistics* 29 (1), 19-51.

Pupko, T., Itsik Pe'er, Ron Shamir, and Dan Graur. 2000. A fast algorithm for joint reconstruction of ancestral amino acid sequences. *Mol. Biol. Evol.*, 17(6):890–896.

Robinson, P. M. W. (1989). The Collation and Textual Criticism of Icelandic Manuscripts (1): Collation. *Literary and Linguistic Computing* 4(2), 99-105.

Robinson, P. and R. J. O'Hara. 1996. Cladistic Analysis of an Old Norse Manuscript Tradition. *Research in Humanities Computing* 4.

Robinson, P., A. Barbrook, N. Blake, and C. Howe. 1998. The Phylogeny of The Canterbury Tales. *Nature,* 394:839.

Roelli, P. and Dieter Bachmann. 2010. Towards Generating a Stemma of Complicated Manuscript Traditions: Petrus Alfonsis Dialogus, *Revue d'histoire des textes*, 5(4):307–321.

Roos, T. and T. Heikkila. 2009. Evaluating methods for computer-assisted stemmatology using artificial benchmark data sets. *Literary and Linguistic Computing*, 24:417–433.

Spencer, M. & Howe, C. J (2004). Collating Texts Using Progressive Multiple Alignment. *Computers and the Humanities* 38, 253-270.

Timpanaro, S (2005). *The Genesis of Lachmann's Method*, (ed. and trans. Glenn W. Most), U. of Chicago Press

West, ML (1973). *Textual Criticism and Editorial Technique*, Stuttgart

Yang, Ziheng. 2007. *PAML 4: phylogenetic analysis by maximum likelihood.* Mol. Biol. Evol., 24(8):1586–1591.

Syntax Matters for Rhetorical Structure: The Case of Chiasmus

Marie Dubremetz
Uppsala University
Dept. of Linguistics and Philology
Uppsala, Sweden
`marie.dubremetz@lingfil.uu.se`

Joakim Nivre
Uppsala University
Dept. of Linguistics and Philology
Uppsala, Sweden
`joakim.nivre@lingfil.uu.se`

Abstract

The chiasmus is a rhetorical figure involving the repetition of a pair of words in reverse order, as in "**all** for **one**, **one** for **all**". Previous work on detecting chiasmus in running text has only considered superficial features like words and punctuation. In this paper, we explore the use of syntactic features as a means to improve the quality of chiasmus detection. Our results show that taking syntactic structure into account may increase average precision from about 40 to 65% on texts taken from European Parliament proceedings. To show the generality of the approach, we also evaluate it on literary text and observe a similar improvement and a slightly better overall result.

1 Introduction

There is a growing interest in applying computational techniques within the field of literature as evidenced by the growth of the digital humanities (Schreibman et al., 2008). This field has very specific demands. Unlike many technical fields, literature requires a serious treatment of non-literal language use and rhetorical figures. One of those figures is the antimetabole, or chiasmus of words, illustrated in Figure 1. It consists in the reuse of a pair of words in reverse order for a rhetorical purpose. It is called 'chiasmus' after the Greek letter χ because of the cross this letter symbolises (see Figure 1).

Identifying identical words is easy for a computer, but locating only repetitions that have a rhetorical purpose is not. Can a computer make this distinction? And if yes, which features should we model

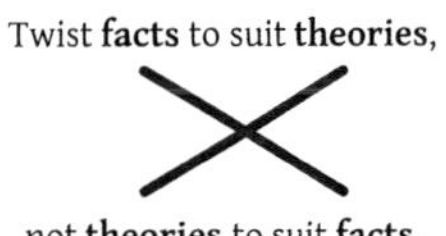

Figure 1: Schema of a chiasmus

for that? This paper presents the first attempt to go beyond shallow surface features in order to detect chiasmus. We start from the shallow feature-based algorithm introduced by Dubremetz and Nivre (2015) and extend it with features based on syntactic structure. We train models on the annotated corpora already used in previous work and evaluate on a new corpus. Our results show that both positive and negative syntactic features can improve the quality of detection, improving average precision by almost 25% absolute compared to a baseline system using only shallow features. As a generalization test, we apply the model trained on political discourse to literary text (the Sherlock Holmes novels and short stories) and obtain an improvement of 17% average precision compared to the baseline.

2 Related Work

Despite a long tradition in rhetorics and linguistics, the terms *chiasmus* and *antimetabole* do not really have clear definitions. In the earliest times, Diderot and D'Alembert (1782) as well as Quintilian (Greene et al., 2012) give us very basic identification features. They talk about the degree of identity that can be accepted to consider two words as identical (strictly identical strings, lemmas or synonyms). On the other hand, Rabatel (2008) and

47

Proceedings of the Fifth Workshop on Computational Linguistics for Literature, NAACL-HLT 2016, pages 47–53,
San Diego, California, June 1, 2016. ©2016 Association for Computational Linguistics

Nordahl (1971) try to find subcategories of chiasmi on a deep semantic basis: for instance chiasmi expressing contrast (Rabatel, 2008). The notion of antimetabole is floating. Dictionaries of stylistics tend to quote the same prototypical chiasmi to illustrate examples, which is not helpful when trying to capture the linguistic variety of chiasmi. The purpose of the linguists is to define chiasmus compared to other figures (for instance chiasmus as opposed to paralellism). To the best of our knowledge there is no pure linguistic study that tries to distinguish between chiasmus and random repetition of words in a criss-cross manner. In non-computer assisted linguistics, as opposed to computational linguistics, rhetoric is taken for granted. Linguistics has to answer only one question: Which figure is instantiated by this piece of rhetoric? Computational linguistics now has to answer not only this question but also the question of whether a piece of text is a piece of rhetoric in the first place.

Gawryjolek (2009) was the first to tackle the automated detection of repetitive figures and of chiasmus in particular. Following the general definition of the figure, he proposed to extract every repetition of words that appear in a criss-cross pattern. Thanks to him, we know that this pattern is extremely frequent while true positive chiasmi are rare. To give an idea of the rarity, Dubremetz and Nivre (2015) give the example of *River War* by Winston Churchill, a book consisting of $150,000$ words, with $66,000$ examples of criss-cross patterns but only one true positive.[1] Hromada (2011) then proposed to add a feature constraint to the detection: he drastically reduced the number of false positives by requiring three pairs of words repeated in reverse order without any variation in the intervening material. Unfortunately, in the example of Churchill's book, this also removes the one true positive and the user ends up with a totally empty output. Finally, Dubremetz and Nivre (2015) built on the intuition of Hromada (2011) and added features to the detection of chiasmus, but in a different way. They observed that chiasmus, like metaphor (Dunn, 2013), is a graded phenomenon with prototypical examples and controversial/borderline cases such as Example 1.

(1) It is just as contrived to automatically allocate **Taiwan** to **China** as it was to allocate **China**'s territory to **Taiwan** in the past.

Thus, chiasmus detection should not be a binary classification task. Instead, Dubremetz and Nivre (2015) argue that a chiasmus detector should extract criss-cross patterns and rank them from prototypical chiasmi to less and less likely instances.

A serious methodological problem for the evaluation of chiasmus detection is the massive concentration of false positives (about $66,000$ of them for only one true positive in $150,000$ words). Such a needle in the haystack problem makes the constitution of an exhaustively annotated corpus extremely time consuming and repetitive to the extreme. This is analogous to the situation in web document retrieval, where the absolute recall of a system is usually not computable, and where recall is therefore measured only relative to the pool of documents retrieved by a set of systems (Clarke and Willett, 1997). The evaluation of Dubremetz and Nivre (2015) is based on the same principle: in a series of experiments their different "chiasmus retrieval engines" return different hits. They annotate manually the top two hundred of those hits and obtain a pool of relevant (and irrelevant) inversions, on which they can measure average precision to show that chiasmi can be ranked using a combination of shallow features like stopwords, conjunction detection, punctuation position, and similarity of n-gram context. The present work goes beyond the idea of Dubremetz and Nivre (2015). We believe that by using structural features defined in terms of part-of-speech tags and dependency structure, we can improve the average precision of chiasmus detection. Therefore, we will reproduce their algorithm and gradually add new features to check on a new corpus if there is any improvement.

3 Ranking Model and Feature Modeling

We reuse the linear model for prediction developed by Dubremetz and Nivre (2015), which allows the addition of any arbitrary features.

$$f(r) = \sum_{i=1}^{n} x_i \cdot w_i$$

---

[1] **Ambition** stirs **imagination** nearly as much as **imagination** excites **ambition**.

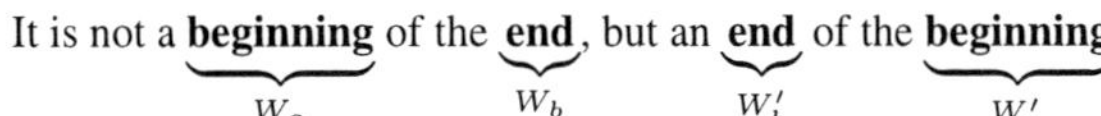

Figure 2: Schema of a chiasmus, W for word.

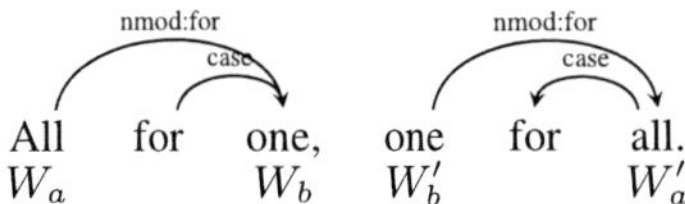

Figure 3: Schematic representation of chiasmus, W for word.

Here r is a string containing a pair of inverted words, x_i is the value of the ith feature, and w_i is the weight associated with this feature. Given two inversions r_1 and r_2, $f(r_1) > f(r_2)$ means that the inversion r_1 is more likely to be a chiasmus than r_2.

3.1 Part-of-Speech Tags

Part-of-speech tagging provides a coarse grammatical analysis of the text, which we can exploit to refine the detection of chiasmus. We model tag features as positive features. Words that are detected in a criss-cross pattern already share the same lemma (base form). As shown in Figure 2, we normally expect W_a to have the same tag as W_a', and W_b the same tag as W_b', unless they are ambiguous words that happen to share the same lemma. Unfortunately, this can be true in false positives too, above all in duplicates.[2] What seems more unique in Figure 2 is that all the main words of the prototypical chiasmus have the same tag, Noun in this case. In our tag-based model, we therefore add a weight of $+10$ for a binary feature that is true only if W_a, W_b, W_b' and W_a' all have the same tag.

3.2 Dependency Structures

To further exploit the syntactic structure of a chiasmus candidate, we add features defined over the dependency structure. Our hypothesis is that these features can be both negative and positive. The idea of using syntax as a positive feature is not hard to motivate. If chiasmus is the figure of symmetry (Morier, 1961, p.113), we should see that in the syntax. Symmetry means not only inversion, but also repetition. In Figure 3, we see that W_b has the same role as W_a' (both are the complement of a noun) in a perfectly symmetrical role switching.

It is perhaps harder to see that syntactic dependencies might also play a role as a negative feature, but we motivate this by the remark of Dupriez (2003, art. Antimetabole):

> Metabole consists in saying the same thing with other words, antimetabole saying something else with the same words.

Dupriez (2003) seem to say that for being prototypical the words sharing the same identity in the chiasmus should not be used to express the same thing. Indeed, in Footnote 1, what makes the quote so rhetorical is the fact that 'imagination' and 'ambition' are not repeated with the same role (subject versus verb complement). Therefore, we assume that if the same word is reused with the same syntactic role it is more likely to be a false positive. Example 2 is a false positive found in an earlier experiment: 'convention' is in both cases the direct object of a verb.

(2) We must call on Cameroon to respect this **convention** and find ways of excluding this **country** and any other **country** which violates the **conventions** which it has signed.

Our syntactic features are summarized in Table 1. These features simply count the number of incoming dependency types (labels) that are shared between two words. For example, in Figure 3: 'one' and 'all' share one dependency type (nmod:for).

4 Experiment

Classical machine learning methods cannot be applied as there is no big corpus of annotated chiasmi. The corpus produced by Dubremetz and Nivre (2015) contains about one thousand examples of false positives for only 31 true positives. Therefore, we decided to tune the weights manually, just like in the previous study(Dubremetz and Nivre, 2015). We use the corpus from Dubremetz and Nivre (2015) as training corpus (used both to create and tune the features) and a new corpus as final test corpus. All the data come from Europarl (Koehn, 2005). The training corpus consists of 4 million words. The test corpus is a distinct extract of 2 million words. To test the generality of the approach, we will then apply

---

[2]For example: "**All** for **one**, **one** for **all**" is a true positive instance, "**All for** one, one **for all**" is a duplicate.

Feature	Description	Weight
$\#\text{sameDep}W_b\ W_a'$	Number of incoming dependency types shared by W_b and W_a'.	$+5$
$\#\text{sameDep}W_a\ W_b$	Same but for W_a and W_b'	$+5$
$\#\text{sameDep}W_a\ W_a'$	Same but for W_a and W_a'	-5
$\#\text{sameDep}W_a\ W_a'$	Same but for W_b and W_b'	-5

Table 1: Dependency features used to rank chiasmus candidates

the trained model also to a corpus of literary text: the Sherlock Holmes stories.

4.1 Implementation

Our program takes as input a text that is lemmatized, tagged and parsed using the Stanford CoreNLP tools (Manning et al., 2014). It outputs a list of sentences containing chiasmi candidates. The system provides two types of information about each candidate: the score given by the combination of features and the main words selected. The score is used to rank the sentences as in a search engine: highly relevant criss-cross patterns at the top, less relevant ones at the bottom. Thanks to the main words selection, a human annotator can see which words the system considered to constitute the criss-cross pattern in the chiasmus and determine whether the candidate is a true positive, a false positive, or a duplicate of a true positive (that is, an instance covering the same text as a true positive but with the wrong words matched). In the evaluation, duplicates are considered as false positives.

4.2 Results and Analysis

To evaluate our features, we reproduce the experiment of Dubremetz and Nivre (2015) which uses only shallow features. Then we add our own features with the weights stated in Section 3. Following the idea of Clarke and Willett (1997, p.186), we annotate only the top 200 candidates in each experiment. We use two annotators for this task and base our evaluation only on the chiasmi that both annotators considered as true: we found 13 of them. We measured the inter-annotator agreement for the true/false classification task (counting duplicates as false) and obtained a kappa score of 0.69, which is usually considered as indicating good agreement.

Our table presents the average precision which is a standard measure in information retrieval (Croft et

Model	Average Precision	Compared to Baseline
Baseline	42.54	NA
Tag features	59.48	+14
Negative dependency features	40.36	-2.2
Pos dep features	62.40	+20
All dependency features	64.27	+22
All features	67.65	+25

Table 2: Average precision for chiasmus detection (test set).

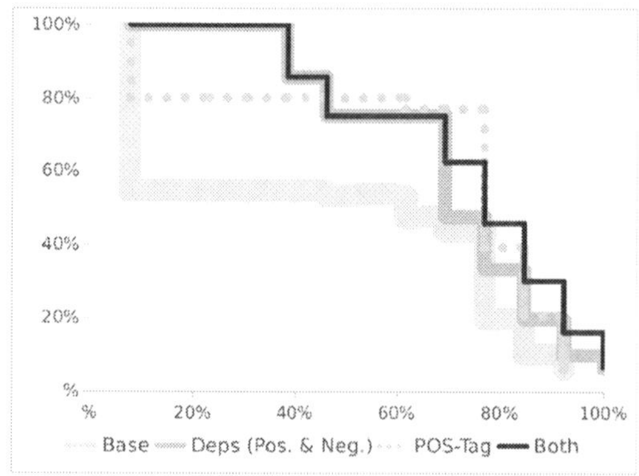

Figure 4: Interpolated precision-recall curve (test set).

al., 2010). It averages over the precision scores at the ranks of the true positives.

In Table 2, we first of all see that tag features add 17% of average precision to the baseline, which shows that the simple idea of requiring tag identity for all words is a powerful way of eliminating false positives. When it comes to dependency features, negative features slightly damage the average precision when used alone (-2.2% compared to the baseline), while positive dependency features give nearly $+20\%$ average precision. However, negative features prove to be useful when combined with the positive features, and when combining both tag and dependency features, we improve by $+25\%$ compared to the baseline.

Combining tag and dependency features not only

improves average precision, but also improves recall compared to the baseline (as well as the system with only dependency features), because it retrieves the following chiasmus (originally ranked below 200):

(3) Do not imagine, however, that **legitimacy** in itself creates **democracy**. Rather, it is **democracy** which creates **legitimacy**.

As can be seen from the precision-recall curve in Figure 4, the combined system also has the most graceful degradation overall, even if it is surpassed by the pure dependency-based system in one region.

Our system definitely proves to be substantially better than the previous state of the art but it has its limits as well: first of all it needs a parsed input and parsing is time consuming. For 2 million words the Stanford CoreNLP takes days to give any output. Once parsed, our system needs 10 minutes per million words in order to output the result. Dependency features do not have the magic ability to get rid of all false positives (otherwise chiasmi like Example3 would be ranked 1 instead of 133 by dependency features). Moreover, syntactic features narrow the type of examples we get: some chiasmi are not based on perfect symmetry of roles and tags. For example:

(4) We must preach for **family values**, and **value families**.

Europarl is a convenient corpus for experimentation: it represents an almost endless source of clean text (more than 45 million words for just the English version), written in a consistent way. Literature is not as convenient: according to the Guiness Book of Records the longest novel ever written is about 1 million words long.[3] So far, our model has been trained on 4 million words and tested on 2 million words from the political discourse genre. We have successfully proven that a model tuned on one Europarl extract can generalise on another Europarl extract. Without any further tuning, can our detector find chiasmi in a different genre?

We chose to answer this by applying it to literary text. Our literature corpus is the complete anthology of Sherlock Holmes stories by Conan Doyle. We download the text file from the internet[4] and did not

___
[3] http://www.guinnessworldrecords.com
[4] https://sherlock-holm.es/stories/plain-text/cano.txt

Model	Average Precision	Diference
Baseline	53.00	NA
All features	70.35	+17

Table 3: Average precision for chiasmus detection (Sherlock Holmes set).

apply any kind of cleaning on it (thus, notes, chapter titles, and tables of content are still remaining). This gave us a corpus of about 650,000 words, to which we applied our baseline model and our final model. In Table 3, we see that the average precision

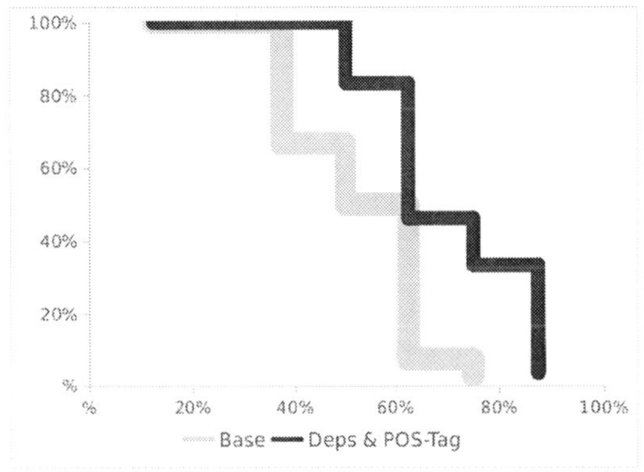

Figure 5: Interpolated precision-recall curve (literature set).

is improved by +17% from the baseline to the final model. On a total of 8 chiasmi, the baseline finds 6 of within 200 candidates whereas our final model finds 7, which means that we improve not only precision but also recall. We can observe this performance on the recall-precision curve Figure 5.

With so small numbers, we cannot be sure that the improvement is significant between the baseline and our system. However, the results show that running our model on a literary corpus can provide a significant help to the human user. Our algorithm with over 70% average precision managed to find 5 chiasmi within the top 10 candidates. This saves a considerable amount of human work, and we got this result without any special tuning or cleaning adapted to this genre.

5 Conclusion

The aim of this paper was to improve the performance of a chiasmus detector. The only existing system was based entirely on shallow features like words and punctuation. We have extended that system with features capturing aspects of syntactic structure and discovered three effective features for chiasmus detection: tag features, positive dependency features and negative dependency features. Moreover, we have shown that the same model works well for literary text. An additional contribution of this paper is the annotation of two new corpora by two annotators. The first one is a Europarl corpus that includes 13 true positives on 466 instances. The second corpus is an anthology of Sherlock Holmes that includes 8 true positives on 399 instances.[5] By adding these to the corpus previously created by Dubremetz and Nivre (2015), we provide a data set that might be large enough to start exploring machine learning instead of tuning feature weights manually.

A   Europarl Chiasmi

1. But if he were alive today, he would have said instead: "**East** is **West**, and **West** is **East**, and never the twain shall part."

2. I can therefore find no reason to differentiate between **Poland** and **Hungary** or between **Hungary** and **Poland**.

3. I should like to conclude by giving you some food for thought: Europe is good at converting **euros** into **research**, but often fails in converting **research** into **euros**, and that must change in future.

4. I think that Parliament is being held hostage to a few Stalinists, who always take a **strong** line with those who are **weak** and are **weak** in the face of those who are **strong**.

5. In turn, defence is constantly changing its boundaries in a world in which the perception of these is ever more blurred: nowadays, we cannot only consider the territorial defence of one State faced with a possible attack by another, but rather, as has been correctly said, we have **armies** that lack clear **enemies** and **enemies** that lack **armies**.

6. It is yet another example of the EU taking money from **poor** people in **rich** countries and giving it to **rich** people in **poor** countries.

7. Many of those areas have over the years turned from **land** into **sea** or from **sea** into **land**, with or without specific human intervention.

8. **Reason** without **passion** is sterile, **passion** without **reason** is heat.

9. We must avoid a situation where no answer is given because a society where **citizens** are afraid of their **institutions** - and perhaps more importantly **institutions** are afraid of their **citizens** - makes for a very weak democracy.

10. We want much greater enlargement, but without providing the corresponding funds and we invent lower and lower cohesion targets along the lines of "if the **mountain** won't come to **Mohammed**, then let's take **Mohammed** to the **mountain**".

11. What we now have to do, once we have consolidated the internal aspects of our project, is turn Europe into an international operator capable of comprehensive action with regard to the challenges facing the world, a world in which nations are too **big** to resolve their **small** problems and too **small** to resolve the **big** problems we are faced with on a global scale.

12. Women, men, workers, students, the unemployed, pacifists and ecologists will no longer be opposing the system but will be terrorists because - as Hegel, then an old man, wrongly said - 'the **real** is **rational** and the **rational real**' , and for our legislators nothing is more real than the present social and economic disorder and nothing is more irrational, and therefore terrorist, than the need to overthrow and eliminate it.

13. Do not imagine, however, that **legitimacy** in itself creates **democracy**. Rather, it is **democracy** which creates **legitimacy**.

B   Sherlock Holmes Chiasmi

1. "After all, since we are to be on such terms, Mr. Altamont," said he, "I don't see why **I** should trust **you** any more than **you** trust **me**."

---

⁵The reader will find in appendix the list of all true positive chiasmi in both of our corpora.

2. "For years **I** have loved **her**. For years **she** has loved **me**."

3. "I don't think you need alarm yourself," said I. "I have usually found that there was **method** in his **madness**." "Some folks might say there was **madness** in his **method**," muttered the Inspector.

4. "But the **Sikh** knows the **Englishman**, and the **Englishman** knows the **Sikh**."

5. "He seems to have declared war on the **King**'s **English** as well as on the **English king**."

6. "I can still remember your complete indifference as to whether the **sun** moved round the **earth** or the **earth** round the **sun**."

7. "Insensibly one begins to twist **facts** to suit **theories**, instead of **theories** to suit **facts**."

8. "He pays me well to **do** my **duty**, and my **duty** I'll **do**."

References

Sarah J. Clarke and Peter Willett. 1997. Estimating the recall performance of Web search engines. *Proceedings of Aslib*, 49(7):184–189.

Bruce Croft, Donald Metzler, and Trevor Strohman. 2010. *Search Engines: Information Retrieval in Practice: International Edition*, volume 54. Pearson Education.

Denis Diderot and Jean le Rond D'Alembert. 1782. *Encyclopédie méthodique: ou par ordre de matières, volume 66*. Panckoucke.

Marie Dubremetz and Joakim Nivre. 2015. Rhetorical Figure Detection: the Case of Chiasmus. In *Proceedings of the Fourth Workshop on Computational Linguistics for Literature*, pages 23–31, Denver, Colorado, USA, June. Association for Computational Linguistics.

Jonathan Dunn. 2013. What metaphor identification systems can tell us about metaphor-in-language. In *Proceedings of the First Workshop on Metaphor in NLP*, pages 1–10, Atlanta, Georgia, June. Association for Computational Linguistics.

Bernard Dupriez. 2003. *Gradus, les procédés littéraires*. Union Générale d'Éditions 10/18.

Jakub J. Gawryjolek. 2009. *Automated Annotation and Visualization of Rhetorical Figures*. Master thesis, Universty of Waterloo.

Roland Greene, Stephen Cushman, Clare Cavanagh, Jahan Ramazani, and Paul Rouzer, editors. 2012. *The Princeton Encyclopedia of Poetry and Poetics: Fourth Edition*. Princeton University Press.

Daniel Devatman Hromada. 2011. Initial Experiments with Multilingual Extraction of Rhetoric Figures by means of PERL-compatible Regular Expressions. In *Proceedings of the Second Student Research Workshop associated with RANLP 2011*, pages 85–90, Hissar, Bulgaria.

Philipp Koehn. 2005. Europarl: A Parallel Corpus for Statistical Machine Translation. In *The Tenth Machine Translation Summit*, pages 79–86, Phuket, Thailand.

Christopher D Manning, Mihai Surdeanu, John Bauer, Jenny Finkel, Steven J Bethard, and David McClosky. 2014. The Stanford CoreNLP Natural Language Processing Toolkit. In *Association for Computational Linguistics (ACL) System Demonstrations*, pages 55–60.

Henri Morier. 1961. *Dictionnaire de poétique et de rhétorique*. Presses Universitaires de France.

Helge Nordahl. 1971. Variantes chiasmiques. Essai de description formelle. *Revue Romane*, 6:219–232.

Alain Rabatel. 2008. Points de vue en confrontation dans les antimétaboles PLUS et MOINS. *Langue française*, 160(4):21–36.

Susan Schreibman, Ray Siemens, and John Unsworth. 2008. *A Companion to Digital Humanities*. John Wiley & Sons, April.

Bilingual Chronological Classification of Hafez's Poems

Arya Rahgozar & Diana Inkpen
SEECS, University of Ottawa
Ottawa, Ontario, Canada
{arahg096,Diana.Inkpen}@uottawa.ca

Abstract

We present a novel task: the chronological classification of Hafez's poems (ghazals). We compiled a bilingual corpus in digital form, with consistent idiosyncratic properties. We have used Hooman's labeled ghazals in order to train automatic classifiers to classify the remaining ghazals. Our classification framework uses a Support Vector Machine (SVM) classifier with similarity features based on Latent Dirichlet Allocation (LDA). In our analysis of the results we use the LDA topics' main terms that are passed on to a Principal Component Analysis (PCA) module.

1   Introduction

Chronological classification of any artwork is a worthwhile task. We focus on the poetry of the giant of Persian poetry, Hafez from Shiraz. The purpose of our automatic chronological classification of Hafez's ghazals is to establish the relative timing of any poem concerning Hafez's lifetime, and thus to help understand his poetry better, while applying a semantic analysis approach. The objective of this research is to classify ghazals using machine learning (ML) techniques with scholarly benefits rooted in literary analysis and hermeneutics.

Harsh political conditions of Hafez's time required a unique type of encryption and mystical quality to the poems. As a result, scholars have argued for centuries about the ghazals' possible interpretations and engaged in enduring polemics over the subject.

We draw on the work of an outstanding author, Dr. Mahmood Hooman. In his seminal book about Hafez from about 80 years ago (Hooman, 1938), he has partially done this chronological classification by hand.

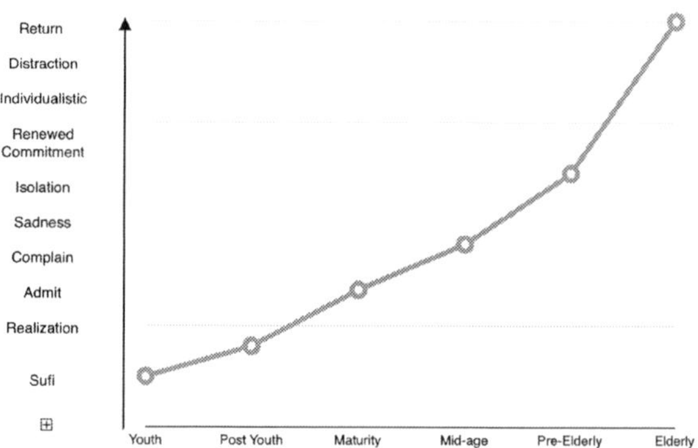

Figure 1: Hafez's Evolutionary Growth Curve

Hooman provides a psychological and personality-growth perspective on the poet Hafez. This perspective plays an integral role in the interpretation of the poems and their chronological classification – see Figure 1. This analytical spectrum of Hafez and his ghazals has been our guidance in deciding to apply Natural Language Processing (NLP) semantic-based methods in the chronological classification of Hafez's ghazals.

We considered the task as a deserving candidate for automatic text classification by ML. From the very beginning, we realized the great challenges involved. Most important, there was no large and reliable corpus of Hafez poems available in electronic form. Therefore we built one composed of all the 468 ghazals, each about 10 lines. We were able to include good English version only for 71 of them.[1]

In addition to classification, we also decided that we need some means of providing an intuitive rationale for each prediction. Therefore, in the end, we applied a Topic-Term analysis to the poems to address that.

---

[1]English translations are by Shahriar Shahriari.

Proceedings of the Fifth Workshop on Computational Linguistics for Literature, NAACL-HLT 2016, pages 54–62,
San Diego, California, June 1, 2016. ©2016 Association for Computational Linguistics

2 Hafez Corpus

We have used Ghazvini's version of Hafez's poems[2] and we followed Hooman's approach. We have also added the English translations whenever available. While typing up the poems, we applied predefined rules to all poems. In other words, we ensured consistency while creating our Hafez corpus. It is one of the attributes of an ancient language such as Persian to be flexible, and to provide freedom and variety of writing options within the same compound terms. This variety comes at the expense of complex computational implications. We had to apply consistency rules so that any current or future parsing of the terms is consistent across all 468 ghazals. We have used multiple types of white spaces to separate or join the one-word terms that we write as counter-intuitive in Persian.[3] In places of potential confusion, we have specified the otherwise unwritten vowels and diacritics inline.

As we see in Figure 1 in the chronological and conceptual poem chart, each poem essentially would reside on a specific curve point depending on its determined point in time, and on its semantic elements, theme and attributes that Hooman detected in the poems. Our corpus follows exactly Hooman's order of ghazals.

We have derived rules from the Persian linguistics, defined procedures and specifications, and applied them to our Persian corpus during its development. From the 468 ghazals, Hooman labeled only 249 with time information. We have consolidated six classes of chronological pairs into three (Youth, Maturity and Senectitude) to facilitate classification experiments, as shown in Table 1 (combining labels a and b into a', c and d into b', and e and f into c').

3 Related Work

The Cross-Language Text Categorization (CLTC) task often concerns categorizing text based on the labeled training data from one language to help to classify text in another language. Popular techniques use the bag-of-word (BOW) method as a base

---

Table 1: Corpus Training Labels

Six Classes		Three Classes
Youth = 38	a	a'
After Youth = 25	b	
Maturity = 79	c	b'
Middle Age = 66	d	
Before Senectitude = 28	e	c'
Senectitude = 13	f	

to classify texts. Researchers obtained varied high accuracies in text classification depending on the task, context and corpus size. One source of differences is in how features are developed and weighted; another is in the learning algorithms. Gliozzo and Strapparava (2006) built common etymological ancestry attributes of words between Italian and English, which were used to train an SVM model in one language to classify text in the other. Latent Semantic Analysis (LSA) (Deerwester et al., 1990) was used to create a deep vector representation of the word-document co-occurrences of shared lexical and etymological attributes. Dumais et al. (1997) found semantic correspondences between languages by using LSA and SVM to create multilingual domain models.

Languages adopt words from each other and adjust them for their purposes, yet maintain their common roots. For example, the words *Check*, *Chess* and *Checkmate* in English correspond to their Persian roots as *Shah* and *mat* in *Shah-mat*. In this way, the two languages preserve strong semantic relations.

Luštrek (2006) has a good discussion and overview of the types of features used in text classification, with a focus on genre detection in text classification. Simonton (1990) present experiments in authorship attribution for poetry analysis and lyrics using shallow features such as part-of-speech (POS) features and function word distribution. Simonton analyzed the 154 sonnets attributed to William Shakespeare. Each sonnet was partitioned into four consecutive units (three quatrains and a couplet), and then a computer tracked down how the number of words, different words, unique words, primary process imagery and secondary process imagery changed within each sonnet unit. He no-

---

[2]Mohammad Ghazvini (1874-1949), an Iranian scholar, corrected and prepared today's most reliable prints of Hafez ghazals.

[3]For example, dânef-âmuz 'student' is one word, but we write it as two in Persian.

ticed a common vocabulary change in the end unit, the couplet. Kim et al. (2011) used deeper features such as the distribution of syntactic constructs in prose to analyze authorship and writing style. Synonyms and hyponyms are also used as features (Scott and Matwin, 1998). The POS proportion of *hapax legomena* per document plus end of line rhyme have been examined as features (Mayer et al., 2008). Hirjee and Brown (2009) showed that a statistical rhyme detector can extract in-line slant rhymes to analyze Rap lyrics.

To approximate publication time of the lyrics and detection of the genre, Fell (2014) used features such as vocabulary, style, semantics, orientation and structure of the song for an SVM classifier.

According to (Zrigui et al., 2012), an LDA-SVM model is the best performing classifier in finding main subject heading of Arabic texts; they compared this top performer with Naive Bayes, SVM and kNN classifiers. Luo and Li (2014) employ a two-phased LDA-SVM model to classify about 20 different newsgroup texts. They used LDA, Probabilistic Latent Semantic Indexing (PLSI), PCA, Hierarchical LDA and SVM to classify such documents.

Razavi and Inkpen (2014) used SVM with multilevel LDA features to classify social media messages and newsgroup texts. In search of an efficient text classification method and following the related works mentioned above, we decided to use SVM (Cortes and Vapnik, 1995), because it is a state-of-the-art classification algorithm (Joachims, 1998).

Orthographic, syntactic and phonemic features were used to classify poems by style (Kaplan and Blei, 2007). In analyzing poems and their aesthetics to reach the semantics of imagery, other researchers employ sound devices such as alliteration, consonance and rhyme (Kao and Jurafsky, 2015). More work uses NER and POS taggers to create features to classify poems by style (Delmonte, 2015). Lou et al. (2015) classified poems into nine classes (Love, Nature, Religion and other), allowing a poem to be in more than one class.

Unlike the previous work on poetry classification, we classify the poems by one poet alone – Hafez – in chronological order, and the poems contain many symbols and hidden semantics that we captured by LDA-driven cosine similarities in vector space.

4 Proposed Methodology

As shown in Figure 2, we used feature-engineering techniques based on Bag-Of-Words[4] and Term Frequency-Inverse Document Frequency (TF-IDF) that we transformed into the vector space of LSI or LDA. We then used those representations for training the SVM classifier. To get our best performing SVM classifier, we used a new representation based on cosine similarity measures calculated from LDA topics. The dictionary maps a poem's normalized words into an index.

Similarly to the work of Bezdek et al. (1998) inspired by (Chang, 1974), we have averaged *Prototype* similarity vectors for each class. That is, each poem has three *Prototype* features to train SVM. We first calculated each poem's similarity to others then we averaged that by class. In other words, each of the three features is the ghazal's average LDA-driven *cosine similarity* to all other poems of each class, calculated one by one, to capture their probabilistic semantic relatedness.

We discuss in section 6 the highest probability terms among all six[5] topics for each class – *Youth*, *Maturity* and *Senectitude*– to analyze the results. We used the GENSIM library (Řehůřek and Sojka, 2010) to develop the features; the similarity features in GENSIM and its indexing mechanism by LSI concepts are based on (Deerwester et al., 1990). Then we use WEKA (Hall et al., 2009) to train the SVM classifier. We grouped the six classes of Hooman into three, for performance reasons. In the source data, wherever available, English translations are directly appended to the poems' Persian instances. Similar to Figure 3, that shows the LDA clusters for each class (only one term from each cluster is shown), we also created the cluster of top terms for predicted poems for error analysis purposes. We compared the associated class terms with those for each predicted class of ghazals to study the internal topic attributes and hence we were able to provide clues for predictions. We hope that the results of our analysis will help NLP researchers to both observe the effects of LDA topic terms in liter-

---

[4]The frequency of each word used as a feature, irrespective of grammar, order or semantic relations.

[5]More LDA topics did not produce any important lift in performance.

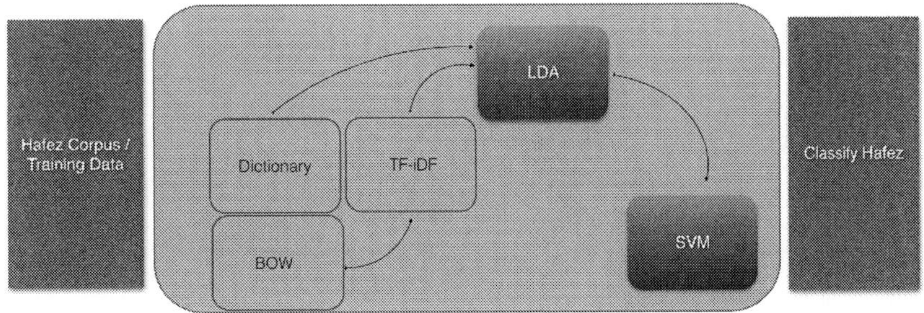

Figure 2: Technical High-level Process

ature contexts and to extend our insight further over the poems of Hafez.

As part of the final analysis of the results, we have used PCA to reduce dimensionality and to draw the LDA results in 2D for analysis purposes. Driven by the LDA model, clusters of words may slightly differ in each run. We were able to show that LDA terms relations by PCA, bring about consistency, relatively maintain comparability of distinctive characteristic of a ghazal and its class for which the prediction is made, and therefore help the user not only better distinguish between the ghazals possible classes but also better justify the classification theme on Hooman's classes. Kaplan and Blei (2007) use PCA so that they can visualize similarity among poems. They use orthographic, syntactic and phonemic features to tackle, distinguish and classify poems by style. Kao and Jurafsky (2015) extended that work and introduced other features of sound devices – such as alliteration, consonance and rhyme – in order to analyze further poems and their aesthetics to get at the semantics of imagism. The cluster of terms caused interesting discussions amongst our experts. Term clusters also played a critical role in providing the rationale for the predictions and their comparisons and interpretations.

5 Experiments and Results

The baseline accuracy for the classification of the three amalgamated classes is 58.2.%[6]

In Table 2, we show the results of tenfold cross-validation for our SVM classifiers with different sets of features. The evaluation measure is the weighted average of the F-measures proportional to the num-

Table 2: SVM Classification Results for 3 classes (F-measure)

Features	Language	
	Persian	Persian-English
BOW	61%	65.1%
LDA	56.2%	58.2%
BOW+LSI	61.4%	65.1%
BOW+LDA	61.8%	65.1%
LDA Similarity	79.52%	78.4%

ber of elements in each of the three classes, as calculated by WEKA.[7]

In our first experiment, we created the BOW training data as input to the SVM classifier and increased the F-measure to 61%. The LDA factors alone did not go above the baseline of 58%. Keeping the BOW and adding the LSI or LDA factors only slightly improved the F-measure over the BOW alone. A t-test showed a 95% confidence that the results improved significantly when we added the English translations.

At that point, we hypothesized that the LSI- or -LDA-driven similarity factors alone should provide us with strong enough training features. Therefore, in the next experiments, we went back and created the SVM training data only with normalized similarity factors, once with LSI and once with LDA. LDA driven similarity factors proved stronger than those of LSI. That is, as we observed the remarkable strength of these features, we only kept the BOW and LDA factors in the similarity factor calculations, in the final SVM training data. Yet this method brought the accuracy of the classifier to our best result of 79.5% using our Persian training dataset.

---

[6]The Baseline is a classifier that always chooses the most frequent class, b', out of the three.

[7]`http://weka.sourceforge.net/doc.dev/weka/classifiers/Evaluation.html`

The English addition, only in this case, reached a plateau. That, we believe, was due to the scarcity of the features – only three.

To analyze the errors made by the classifier, we looked at the confusion matrix with columns showing the "classified as". We noticed that the classifications faults were often caused by classes a' and c', which make up the smaller sections of the corpus; they are under-represented:

a'	b'	c'	
44	19	0	a'
0	145	0	b'
17	15	9	c'

We have also used the trained model for predicting the classes of the unlabelled ghazals. We then asked our two experts, who consistently validated the labelling results, for a few of the unlabelled ghazals.

6 Analysis of the Results

We only discuss the main term from each of the 6 LDA topics of each class.[8] In the next analysis, we will look at how they correspond each of the top LDA terms of a sample poem from each class. For brevity, we only show one poem per class but in fact the framework proved useful in providing us with insightful clues and consistent intuitive reasoning behind the classifier predictions.

6.1 First Period - Youth

The Youth class has the following cluster of terms:[9]

0. Vision *nazar*, Connected *vasl*, Unable *nâtavan*, Complain *ʃekâyat*, Your Sorrow *qamat*, A Heart *deli*, Glass *ʃıʃə*, Repentance *tobæ*, Universe *jahan*, Hand *dast*.

1. Other *degar*, Flower *gol*, Remenisance *bovad yâd*, Airy *havâi*, Solution *tadbır*, Jam *jam*, Wine *məɪ*, Guru *pır*, Hand *dast*.

2. Is *ast*, From *ke az*, Sorrow *qam*, Be *bâʃ*, There *ânja*, In *andar*, Blood *xʊn*, Wine *mɛy*, Full *por*, To Be Me *bâʃam*.

3. Arch *tâq*, Gem *laæl*, Because *bahrɛ*, You *to*, Face *didɛ*, Speech *ʃirin-soxan*, Limit *hadd*,

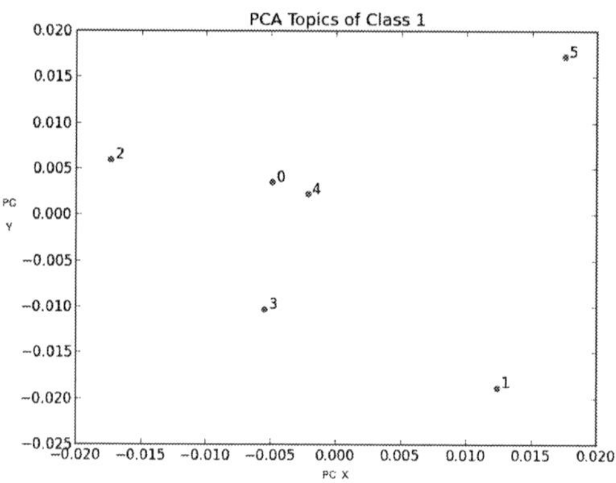

Figure 3: LDA topics for the class Youth

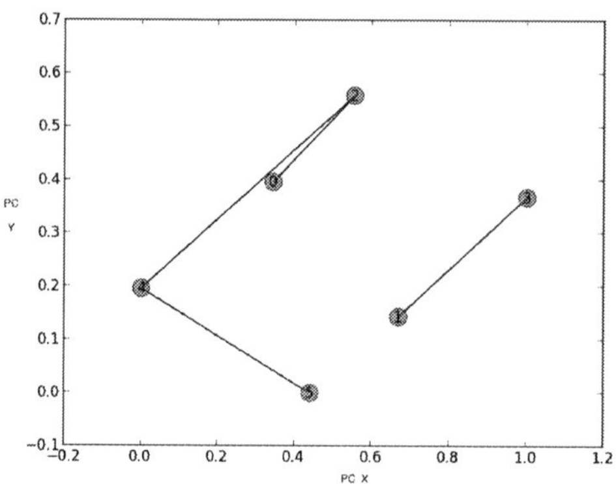

Figure 4: LDA Topics; Graph Relations for the class Youth

Business *kâr*, No Hint *nemibinam-neʃân*, Ruined *xarâb*.

4. Secret *sərr*, Destiny *qadar*, Say *gʊ*, Cup *jâm*, Know *dânı*, Friends *yârân*, Came *âmad*, Dawn *sahar*, Life jân.

5. Break *beʃkan-bɛ*, Title *maqâm*, Life *jân*, Thousands *ɦezârân*, Loose *sost*, Candle *ʃamæ*, My Heart *delam*, Love *əʃq*, Downhill *naʃib*.

6.1.1 Analysis of poems: Class Youth

Let us look at a poem that Hooman has classified as belonging to the Youth period of Hafez's life (and for which the prediction was also the Youth class). Let us observe what elements and cluster of words we see in the ghazal. Here is the first line of the ghazal 48:[10]

---

[8]We experimented with multiple LDA topic numbers but here we only show the results for the Six-Topic top terms for each class and each individual ghazal for comparison.

[9]Persian words in the phonetic form are in italics.

[10]It is 48 according to Hooman's numbering system.

sahargah rahrovi dar sarzamini - hami goft in moamma ba qarini

and the translation of the ghazal is as follows:

A traveler in a strange land Took a stranger by the hand

You will only see clarity of the wine If for forty days you let it stand.

God keep us from the dervish's cloak That conceals an idol in every strand.

Though virtue needs no recognition Let helping the needy be your errand.

O you the owner of the harvest Keep your harvesters from reprimand.

Where has all the joy gone? Why is the pain of love so bland?

Every chest is gloomy dark and sad; Let love's flame in hearts be fanned.

Without the finger of lovers For golden rings there's no demand.

Though Beloved seems to be so harsh The lover accepts every command.

Walk to the tavern and I will ask Have you seen the end you have planned?

Neither Hafiz's heart is in lessons so grand Nor the teacher can fully understand.

By looking at this ghazal,[11] one can observe that the terms *Glass*, *Heart* and *Sorrow* correspond with topic 0. *Sorrow* also belongs to topic 2, but from topic 2, we also have *Is* occurring twice and *Be* is present 5 times. Interestingly enough, the network in Figure 4 shows that there is a relationship between topics 0 and 2. Elements of topics 1 and 5 are depicted as far from topics 2 and 0 in the PCA chart, and accordingly they are not present. Overall, the elements and genre of the ghazal are very consistent with the concepts depicted by the word clusters and topic charts of this class.

As we observe in Figure 3, topics 1, 2 and 5 are the farthest from each other, but in the network or the weighted-Euclidian-distance Figure 4, topics 1 and 3 have no relations with others in the graph. Topics 0, 2, 4 and 5 are related, in that order. These links indicate how the term characteristics of the topics interrelate. In this case, we are more likely to see topics 1 and 3 show up in a ghazal; but the cluster

---

¹¹ We generated the topic terms using the Persian corpus, so the exact term may not necessarily exist in this poetic translation by Shahriar Shahriari.

of words in topics 1 and 2 are hardly expected to show up in the same ghazal. One can also observe the contrast between the two topics 1 and 2; that is, the topic 1 is obviously more positive than topic 2.

6.2 Second Period: Maturity

The Maturity class has the following cluster of terms:

0. Objective *hâjat*, Dust *xâk*, Hafez *hâfez*, Grace *mǝnnat*, Excited *barafruxtǝh*, Palate *kâm*, Heart *del*, That *kǝ*, Concern *kâr*.
1. Vision *nazar*, Life *jân*, Return *baz*, Universe *jahan*, Cleanliness *taharat*, Is *st*, Secret *serr*, So *ke*, Is *ast*.
2. Hafez *hâfez*, Heart *del*, Soleiman *soleimân*, Virtue *honar*, Word *soxan*, Distressed *pariʃân*, See *bin*, Where *kojâ*, Candle *ʃamæ*, Vision *nazar*.
3. Went *raft*, Return *bâz*, Not Remain *namânad*, Flower *gol*, You *to*, Sweetheart *yâr*, When *kǝy*, Harm *balâ*, Sympathy *deli*.
4. Envy *hasrat*, and *va*, Said *goftâ*, That *kæ*, Dust *xâk*, This way *kɛ-ɪn*, Cup *jâm*, Palate *kâm*, come I said *âyad-goftam*, Come *biâ*.
5. I want *xâham*, Has Left *nahâdæ*, Cannot *natavân*, Wrong *qalat*, Eye *çaʃm*, Contract *ahd*, Is-Not *nist*, Wine *mǝy*.

6.2.1 Analysis of poems: Class Maturity

An example of analysis of this section is ghazal 206 of Hooman's classification labeled Maturity. The first line of this ghazal starts with this: *salha dafter ma dar geroye sahba bʊd - ronaghe meikade az darso daaye ma bʊd.*

The translation of the ghazal is as follows:
For years to the red wine my heart was bound The Tavern became alive with my prayer and my sound.
See the Old Magi's goodness with us the drunks Saw whatever we did in everyone beauty had found.
Wash away all our knowledge with red wine Firmaments themselves the knowing minds hound.
Seek that from idols O knowing heart Said the one whose insights his knowledge crowned.
My heart like a compass goes round and round I'm lost in that circle with foot firmly on the ground.
Minstrel did what he did from pain of Love Lashes of wise-of-the-world in their bloody tears have

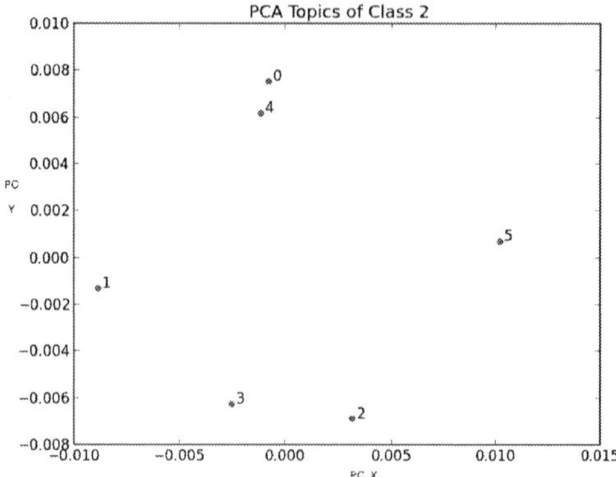

Figure 5: LDA topics for the class Maturity

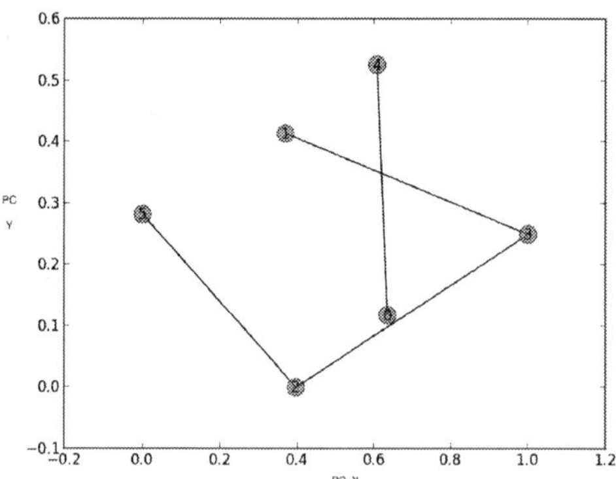

Figure 6: LDA Topics, Graph Relations for the class Maturity

drowned.

With joy my heart bloomed like that flower by the stream Under the shade of that tall spruce myself I found.

My colourful wise Master in my dealings with the black robes My meanness checked and bound else my stories would astound.

Hafiz's cloudy heart in this trade was not spent This merchant saw and heard every hidden sight and sound.

We observe in Figure 5 that the highest number of terms in the term cluster belongs to topics 0 and 4. The term *That* occurs 5 times and 2 times in slightly different form, *Heart* and *Said* are common on topics 0 and 4. The system depicted this relation by both the topics chart and network distance relation charts. Then we observe the terms *Vision* and *Universe* from topic 1 and the term *See* from topic 2 and the term *Flower* from topic 3, each once. Network Figure 6 depicts this relation.

6.3 Third Period: Senectitude

The Senectitude class has the following cluster of terms:

0. Prescription *davâ*, Universe *donyâ*, Does it *bekonad-ze*, Wonder *ajab*, Happy *xoʃ*, Kindness *mɘhr*, Cup *jâm*, Is *bovad*, Veil *hejâb*, Free *rahâ*.

1. Life *jân*, Song *âvâz*, That from *kaz*, Scream *faryâd*, All *fiamæ*, In *andar*, Nightingale *bolbol*, Universe *jahân*, Let it become *ʃavad*.

2. Full *por*, And *va*, That-this *kɪn*, Sadness *qam*,

That *ke*, Became *bɘʃod*, Witness *ʃâhed*, Wine *mɛy*.

3. Word *soxan*, Sun *xorʃid*, Can *tavâni*, Is Not *nabovad*, Light *çerâq*, Is going *miravad*, Monastry *somɘæ*, Nice *neku*, Is not *st-na*, You to.

4. Fell off *oftâd-az*, Fell *oftâd*, My heart *delam*, Blood *xʊn*, Does from *konad-zɘ*, Hand *dast*, Universe *jahân*, Love *ɘʃq*, Familiar *ahl*, Smell *bʊyɘ*.

5. Better *behtar*, Wisdom *aql*, Turn *nɔbat*, Is *st*, Drink *bâdeh*, Within *andar*, To *râ*, Wine *mɘy*, From that *kaz*.

6.3.1 Analysis of poems: Class Senectitude

We have randomly chosen ghazal 241, which Hooman classifies into the last class. It starts with the line: *har chand piro khaste delo natavan shodam - har gah ke yade rʊye to kardam, javan shodam.*

The translation of the poem is as follows:

Though I am old and decrepit and weak My youth returns to me every time your name I speak.

Thank God that whatever my heart ever desired God gave me that and more than I ever could seek.

O young flower benefit from this bounty In this garden I sing through a canary's beak.

In my ignorance I roamed the world at first In thy longing I have become wise and meek.

Fate directs my path to the tavern in life Though many times I stepped from peak to peak.

I was blessed and inspired on the day That at the abode of the Magi spent a week.

In the bounty of the world await not your fate I found

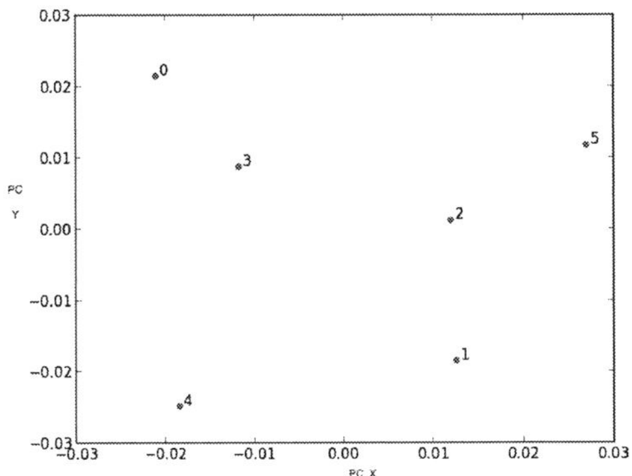

Figure 7: LDA topics for the class Senectitude

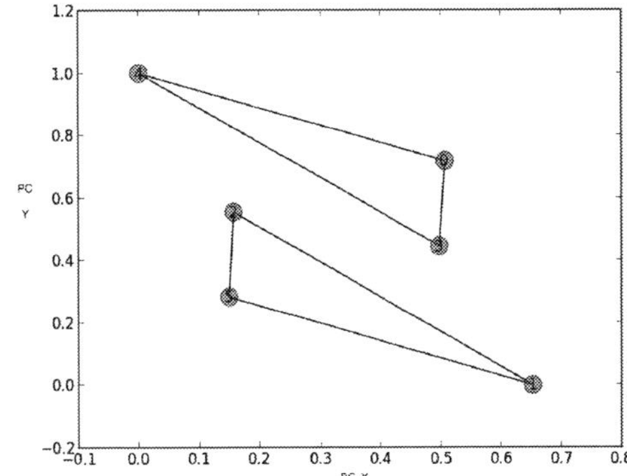

Figure 8: LDA Topic, Graph Relations for the class Senectitude

the Beloved when of wine began to reek.
From the time I was entrapped by thy eyes I was saved from all traps and paths oblique.
The old me befriended the unreliable moon Passage of time is what makes me aged and weak.
Last night came good news that said O Hafiz I forgive all your errs even though may be bleak.

Obviously, this is in agreement with Hooman's descriptions of the attributes of this class, as it shows a very introvert and sad poet who has fewer connections with this natural world. It has specific mentions of Hafez referring to himself as being old. Let us see how our developed cluster of terms plays out in this case.

Consistent with Figure 7, although we see the sporadic presence of nearly all topic terms except that of topic 5, we see that topic 2 is dominant, as we observe and identify the associated cluster of terms of this group such as *That*, three times, *Sad* and *Wine*. The next topic is topic 1 with the terms *Nightingale*, *Universe* and *That-From*.

We observe the terms *My Heart* and *Universe* of topic 4, *Cup* of topic 0 and *Wine* and *Is* of topic 5; but *Wine* also overlaps with topic 2. The term *You* of topic 3 shows up three times.

The interesting symmetric nature of the relation network Figure 8 for this class is consistent with our observation that we have a strong presence of the clusters of terms 1, 2 and 5 and a weaker presence of topics 0, 3 and 4 in which the term *Universe* is common! If we exclude the term *Universe* from both sub-graph terms, looking at the network Figure 8, there are only three distinct terms in the weaker group (0,3,4) compared to the other sub-graph (1,2,5) with term presence of 7.

7 Conclusion and Future Work

Our model automated the classification of Hafez's ghazals using our Hafez corpus. We used LDA and SVM to detect the semantics of Hafez's ghazals and to classify them chronologically. In future work, we will use automatic translations, and will add features such as word embeddings to improve the classification. We are planning to add word-embedding features to enhance our training data and try it with all six Hooman classes. We hope that by increasing the number of features in the training data set we can further improve the more granular classification performance. PCA helped with the intuitive analysis and validation of the prediction results but it deserves a whole paper dedicated to it. We will present more rigorous visualization of topic term validation methods. Another direction of future work is to automatically detect earlier poets' style and rhythms, given the fact that Hafez represents the apex of Persian poetry after *saːdi*, *xâqâni*, *dehlavi* and others. Ashoori (2011) strongly believes that we can even find obvious influences of important books such as *mersad-ol-ebad* and *kaſfol-asrâr*. It would be worthwhile to use ML to draw relations, detect and rank such traces in Hafez's poetry and its hermeneutics.

Acknowledgments

Heartfelt thanks to Mr. Mehran Rahgozar for his continuous expert advice, comprehensive support and considerations with the preparation of the Hafez corpus and implementation of its linguistic properties and literary evaluation of predicted poems. Our special gratitude also extends to Mr. Mehran Raad for his inspiring literary conversations about Hafez and expert advice in the evaluation of the results. We thank the reviewers for their most helpful comments.

References

Dariush Ashoori. 2011. *Erfan o Rendi in Hafez Poetry*. BBC Interview.

James C Bezdek, Thomas R Reichherzer, Gek Sok Lim, and Yianni Attikiouzel. 1998. Multiple-Prototype Classifier Design. *Systems, Man, and Cybernetics, Part C: Applications and Reviews, IEEE Transactions on*, 28(1):67–79.

Chin-Liang Chang. 1974. Finding Prototypes for Nearest Neighbor Classifiers. *Computers, IEEE Transactions on*, 100(11):1179–1184.

Corinna Cortes and Vladimir Vapnik. 1995. Support-Vector Networks. *Machine learning*, 20(3):273–297.

Scott Deerwester, Susan T Dumais, George W Furnas, Thomas K Landauer, and Richard Harshman. 1990. Indexing by Latent Semantic Analysis. *Journal of the American society for information science*, 41(6):391.

Rodolfo Delmonte. 2015. Visualizing Poetry with SPARSAR–Visual Maps from Poetic Content. *Workshop on Computational Linguistics for Literature*, pages 68–78.

Susan T Dumais, Todd A Letsche, Michael L Littman, and Thomas K Landauer. 1997. Automatic Cross-language Retrieval Using Latent Semantic Indexing. In *AAAI spring symposium on cross-language text and speech retrieval*, volume 15, pages 15–21.

Michael Fell. 2014. Lyrics Classification. Master's thesis, Saarland University.

Alfio Gliozzo and Carlo Strapparava. 2006. Exploiting Comparable Corpora and Bilingual Dictionaries for Cross-language Text Categorization. In *Proceedings of the 21st International Conference on Computational Linguistics and the 44th annual meeting of the Association for Computational Linguistics*, pages 553–560. Association for Computational Linguistics.

Mark Hall, Eibe Frank, Geoffrey Holmes, Bernhard Pfahringer, Peter Reutemann, and Ian H Witten. 2009. The WEKA Data Mining Software: an Update. *ACM SIGKDD explorations newsletter*, 11(1):10–18.

Hussein Hirjee and Daniel G Brown. 2009. Automatic Detection of Internal and Imperfect Rhymes in Rap Lyrics. In *ISMIR*, pages 711–716.

Mahmood Hooman. 1938. *Hafez*. Tahuri.

Thorsten Joachims. 1998. Text Categorization with Support Vector Machines: Learning with Many Relevant Features. In Claire Nédellec and Céline Rouveirol, editors, *European Conference on Machine Learning (ECML)*, pages 137–142, Berlin. Springer.

Justine T Kao and Dan Jurafsky. 2015. A Computational Analysis of Poetic Style. *LiLT (Linguistic Issues in Language Technology)*, 12(3):1–33.

David M Kaplan and David M Blei. 2007. A Computational Approach to Style in American Poetry. In *Data Mining, 2007. ICDM 2007. Seventh IEEE International Conference on*, pages 553–558. IEEE.

Sangkyum Kim, Hyungsul Kim, Tim Weninger, Jiawei Han, and Hyun Duk Kim. 2011. Authorship Classification: a Discriminative Syntactic Tree Mining Approach. In *Proceedings of the 34th international ACM SIGIR conference on Research and development in Information Retrieval*, pages 455–464. ACM.

Andres Lou, Diana Inkpen, and Chris Tanasescu. 2015. Multilabel Subject-Based Classification of Poetry. In *The Twenty-Eighth International Flairs Conference*.

Le Luo and Li Li. 2014. Defining and Evaluating Classification Algorithm for High-dimensional Data Based on Latent Topics. *PloS one*, 9(1):e82119.

Mitja Luštrek. 2006. Overview of Automatic Genre Identification. *Ljubljana, Slovenia: Jožef Stefan Institute, Department of Intelligent Systems*.

Rudolf Mayer, Robert Neumayer, and Andreas Rauber. 2008. Rhyme and Style Features for Musical Genre Classification by Song Lyrics. In *ISMIR*, pages 337–342.

Amir H Razavi and Diana Inkpen. 2014. Text Representation Using Multi-level Latent Dirichlet Allocation. In *Advances in Artificial Intelligence*, pages 215–226. Springer.

Radim Řehůřek and Petr Sojka. 2010. Software Framework for Topic Modelling with Large Corpora. In *LREC2010 Proceedings*. University of Malta, May.

Sam Scott and Stan Matwin. 1998. Text classification using WordNet Hypernyms. In *Use of WordNet in natural language processing systems: Proceedings of the conference*, pages 38–44.

Dean Keith Simonton. 1990. Lexical Choices and Aesthetic Success: A Computer Content Analysis of 154 Shakespeare Sonnets. *Computers and the Humanities*, 24(4):251–264.

Mounir Zrigui, Rami Ayadi, Mourad Mars, and Mohsen Maraoui. 2012. Arabic Text Classification Framework Based on Latent Dirichlet Allocation. *CIT. Journal of Computing and Information Technology*, 20(2):125–140.